EXECUTIVE MIGRATION

THE FLORIDA RELOCATION PLAYBOOK

JOE SCHORR

Executive Migration: The Florida Relocation Playbook

Plan Your Move Like a CEO, Not a Snowbird.

Published by Wizzo Press, Tampa, FL

ISBN: 979-8-9936496-3-4

eISBN: 979-8-9936496-2-7

For permissions, speaking, or consulting inquiries:

Joe@Wizzo.Group

First Edition | November 2025

Printed in the United States of America

Wizzo Press and the Wizzo goose logo are trademarks of the Wizzo Group, LLC.

DEDICATION

To my Tara,
the one who ALWAYS believes,
with unlimited love and support.

and

To my children,
now starting families of their own.
My raison d'être.

INTRODUCTION

WHY MOVING TO FLORIDA ISN'T JUST A CHANGE OF ADDRESS. IT'S A BUSINESS DECISION

At some point in every executive's career, you start to feel a shift. It's not just about the job anymore, it's about the trade-off between what you're earning and what it's costing you to keep earning it.

The long hours, the traffic, the taxes, the cold. The creeping sense that you're working harder to keep less. Then one day, it clicks: *If I ran my life the way I run my business, I'd move.*

That moment is where this book begins.

I wrote: **Executive Migration: The Florida Relocation Playbook** for leaders who think in terms of ROI, strategy, and optimization, but are now applying those same instincts to their personal lives. For many, Florida has become the natural next step. It's not just the sunshine. It's the freedom, the math, and the momentum. The state has quietly turned into the operating capital of America's new executive class; the founders, investors, and technologists who've traded city skylines for waterfront Wifi and a tax code that doesn't penalize success.

But relocating isn't as simple as changing zip codes. It's a full-scale transformation of how you live, work, and think.

The mistake most people make is treating relocation like a real estate transaction. They pick a house, call a mover, and hope everything else falls into place. But for executives, a move has far deeper implications. It affects your equity events, your tax domicile, your network, your team structure, your time with family, and even how your next opportunity finds you.

Think of relocation as a **re-platforming**, the same way a company migrates its tech stack to something faster, leaner, and more scalable. You're moving the system that runs your life. And just like in business, timing, structure, and execution matter.

Over the next ten chapters, we'll build a playbook that helps you treat your relocation like a strategic initiative. You'll learn how to measure your **Relocation ROI** (financial and lifestyle), prove your **domicile** the right way, align your **timing** with your financial calendar, and find the region that matches your professional pace. You'll see how to rebuild your network from scratch, evaluate advisors, and design the kind of Florida life that's not just relaxed, but optimized.

Each chapter ends with a short **Action Plan** five or six steps you can actually take. These are your "next move" prompts: things to calculate, conversations to start, documents to update, and habits to build. They'll also feed into a separate workbook for those who want to turn their relocation into a project plan rather than a wish list.

This isn't a book about real estate. It's about **re-engineering your operating system**. Aligning your income, identity, and environment so you can keep building without burning out.

If you're reading this, you've already done the hard part: you built something worth protecting. Now it's time to build the life around it.

Welcome to your next chapter. One where you don't just move to Florida. You move like a founder.

A NOTE ON PERSPECTIVE

I've spent 30 years in Florida while working at the C-suite level with executives globally. Most recently, I've served as Chief Revenue Officer of a cybersecurity company and founded Wizzo Group, advising on strategy, partnerships, and go-to-market architecture. But I'm also a licensed Florida Real Estate Agent.

This combination of Florida market experience and executive operations informs the frameworks in this book. The patterns I've observed over three decades; which executives thrive here, which struggle, and why, shape the practical guidance you'll find in each chapter.

HOW TO USE THIS BOOK

Think of this book as your pre-planning guide. Before you start looking at properties, before you call a moving company, even before you've fully decided to make this move… this book helps you think through the strategic questions that most people only consider after it's too late to optimize.

You can read it straight through as a narrative, or you can use it as a reference guide, jumping to the chapters that address your current questions.

Each chapter ends with an **Action Plan**; specific exercises, worksheets, and prompts that turn concepts into action. These aren't just ideas to consider. They're work to do. If you complete the Action Plans as you go, you'll have built a comprehensive relocation strategy by the time you finish the book.

If you're working with the companion **Workbook Edition**, you'll find expanded versions of these exercises with more space for reflection, planning, and tracking your progress.

The chapters build on each other:

- **Chapters 1-2** help you decide if this move makes sense and how to measure its value

- **Chapters 3-4** focus on the technical side: domicile and timing
- **Chapters 5-6** help you choose your market and build your network
- **Chapters 7-8** cover property strategy and advisor selection
- **Chapters 9-10** help you operationalize your new life and design for freedom

By the end, you won't just know how to move to Florida. You'll know how to build a Florida life that compounds in value every year.

ONE MORE THING

Throughout this book, I'll be straight with you about something: working with the right advisor matters enormously for executive relocations.

Not because the transaction is complicated (though it can be), but because the strategic decisions around that transaction affect everything else: your taxes, your network, your domicile, your family integration, and your long-term ROI.

When you see moments in this book where I talk about advisor selection, or where I explain why certain approaches work better than others, know that this comes from three decades of watching executives either get this right or learn expensive lessons.

I'm not going to pretend I'm objective. I believe strongly that executives need advisors who understand both the real estate market AND the executive world. That combination is rare, and when you find it, it's worth building a relationship around.

Whether you work with me or someone else who brings that same combination of market knowledge and executive understanding, get this part right. The difference between the right advisor and the wrong one isn't just money, it's whether your Florida life actually delivers the freedom and ROI you moved here to create.

Now let's build your playbook.

THE GREAT TECH MIGRATION

WHY EVERYONE YOU KNOW IS MOVING SOUTH

WHEN I FIRST STARTED NOTICING THE pattern, it wasn't in headlines. It was in text messages.

A VP of Product from Philly asking how hard it really was to buy in St. Pete. A cybersecurity founder from Boston who wanted to know if you could still get good engineers in Tampa Bay. A CFO from New York asking about private schools and airports.

Then it became a steady rhythm: "Thinking of moving south. You happy you did it?"

That's the quiet start of almost every migration wave. It begins with whispers among peers before it ever hits the data.

Executives, especially in tech, are a mobile species. We chase opportunity, not geography. But something shifted after 2020. The world didn't just decentralize work; it decentralized ambition. The "tech capitals" stopped feeling like the only place you could build something meaningful. The cost of staying in them started to outweigh the upside.

California's tax rate didn't change overnight, but the tolerance for it did. The value of proximity, the belief that you needed to be two blocks from your Series B investor or that your kid's school had to be in Palo Alto, started to erode. Once people realized they could build, lead, and scale from anywhere with strong wifi, the map opened up.

Florida, for a lot of us, wasn't just a financial decision. It was a return to agency.

THE SHIFT FROM ESCAPE TO STRATEGY

There's a difference between running away and moving forward. The people who relocate here with purpose treat it like a business strategy, not a getaway plan.

Florida has been framed for decades as the place where people retire, not where they reload. But that narrative doesn't hold anymore. The state has quietly built the infrastructure, community, and energy that modern operators need. Airports that connect globally, cities that foster innovation, and tax policies that actually reward effort.

I've watched this transformation over three decades. When I moved to Florida in the mid-1990s, the conversation was different. Tech executives didn't come here. They went to Silicon Valley, Boston, or Austin. Florida was where you went when you were done building.

Now? Tampa International Airport connects to 90+ destinations. St. Petersburg's Innovation District houses dozens of tech companies. Miami's Brickell district rivals Manhattan for deal flow. The narrative has completely flipped.

What's drawn senior talent isn't just the zero income tax. It's the psychological relief of operating without friction.

Think about how much of your professional life revolves around reducing drag. You optimize meetings, teams, platforms, and budgets. Yet most executives accept lifestyle friction as "just the cost of doing business." Long commutes, high taxes, tight housing, endless overhead.

When you start looking at your life through the same optimization lens you apply to your company, relocation becomes the logical next project.

The smartest people I know didn't move because they were angry. They moved because they saw a better model.

THE NUMBERS BEHIND THE WAVE

Let me give you a sense of what this migration actually looks like, beyond the anecdotes.

In 2023, Florida added more than 365,000 new residents, more than any other state. But here's what the headlines miss: it's not just volume, it's composition. The people moving aren't retirees anymore. They're working professionals, and increasingly, they're high earners.

In Tampa Bay specifically, I've watched the median home price in desirable neighborhoods like Hyde Park and South Tampa increase 40% between 2020 and 2024. Not because of speculation, but because executives started discovering what locals have known for years: this is a serious business market that happens to have great weather.

St. Petersburg went from "Tampa's beach town" to a tech hub with its own identity. Companies like Jabil, Raymond James, and Tech Data were always here, but now they're joined by remote-first startups, satellite offices for West Coast companies, and a growing angel investor community.

The pattern I saw in the 1990s and 2000s was corporations relocating headquarters for tax benefits. The pattern I'm seeing now is different: it's individual executives making personal optimization decisions and bringing their networks with them. That creates a very different kind of ecosystem.

A NEW HUB FOR THE BUILDER CLASS

The "builder class" - founders, operators, investors, and senior leaders, are increasingly concentrated around a few lifestyle-first business ecosystems. Florida has become one of them, not by accident, but because it fits the new operating thesis of modern work: live well, build lean, connect widely.

Miami captured early attention because of capital flow and culture. If you're raising a fund or building something that needs constant visibility, Miami's energy is magnetic. I've watched it transform from a Latin American business gateway into a legitimate tech hub over the past five years.

Tampa Bay has become what I call "the operator's market." You'll still find ambition, venture activity, and a growing tech corridor, but the rhythm is different. Conversations last longer. Introductions feel warmer. The energy is serious but sustainable.

I can tell you from three decades here: Tampa Bay is where executives come when they want to build without the noise. You can run a national company from here and still make every family dinner. Flights are easy, housing is sane, and the ocean is close enough to reset your brain after a long week.

Jacksonville is emerging as a logistics and finance hub, less sexy than Miami or Tampa, but with solid fundamentals and lower costs. Orlando, surprisingly, is turning into a remote-work satellite for major companies with families in tow. The theme parks get the headlines, but there's a serious healthcare and simulation tech ecosystem that most people miss.

What unites all of these markets is momentum. In each of them, you'll find founders still building in their garages. Except now the garages overlook water and the burn rate is lower. Engineers who log off at five and take their kids paddleboarding. Investors who run funds from converted bungalows instead of corner offices.

Florida's economy has diversified, but what's changed most is who's steering it. It's not retirees anymore; it's active capital and active leadership.

WHY THE MIGRATION STUCK

Every trend has a half-life. The early pandemic exodus was a mix of panic and novelty. But what stuck after the dust settled were the executives who built real systems around their relocation. Who treated it like a playbook, not an escape hatch.

They changed domicile properly. They built new networks. They realigned their tax, legal, and equity structures. They didn't just move their furniture; they moved their foundation.

That's the key difference between migration and motion. One is sustainable, the other is emotional.

When you treat relocation like an operational upgrade, it becomes one of the most valuable decisions of your career. It's not a reset; it's a reallocation of capital, time, energy, and future upside.

RELOCATION AS A KPI

When you sit in the C-suite long enough, you start to measure everything. Cost per hire. Customer acquisition cost. Burn rate. Churn. But few executives ever measure *personal burn rate*.

Your own energy, time, and income-to-lifestyle ratio are the metrics that silently decide how long you can keep operating at this level.

That's what this move is really about… reclaiming your personal P&L.

When I talk with other executives who've made the move, the conversations sound less like "we moved to the beach" and more like "I optimized my life." They talk about getting time back, about feeling sharper, about being able to think again.

You don't realize how much cognitive overhead you carry until you remove it. The simple act of not worrying about state taxes, or of living where you can see the horizon every day, starts to compound. You stop grinding and start operating with intention again.

That's not just quality of life. That's output optimization.

THE TWO LENSES OF EVERY MOVE

Every relocation decision, at least for someone who thinks in business terms, runs through two lenses: **the financial** and **the functional**.

The financial lens is easy to quantify: income tax, cost of living, property values, capital gains, estate implications. That's the math everyone talks about at dinner.

The functional lens is harder to calculate: access to peers, new business ecosystems, the way your day feels when you wake up. But that's the side that determines whether the move actually sticks.

When you get both right, something remarkable happens. The move becomes additive instead of disruptive. Your life and your work stop competing and start compounding.

The most successful relocations I've seen are the ones where people design around integration, not isolation. They pick a place that supports who they are, not just what they earn. They think about schools, communities, venture access, and travel hubs with the same care they use to choose investors or partners.

Three Executive Profiles

Let me show you what this actually looks like through three real patterns I've observed (names and details changed, but the archetypes are real):

Profile 1: The CTO Who Optimized for Focus

David was CTO of a Series B SaaS company based in San Francisco. Fully remote company, but he was still paying California income tax on his $400K salary plus equity. More importantly, he was exhausted.

The city energy that used to fuel him now drained him. Every coffee meeting turned into three. Every networking event felt performative. He needed space to think.

He moved to St. Petersburg in 2022, bought a house in the Old Northeast neighborhood (walkable, quiet, close to downtown but not tourist-heavy), and built a home office that overlooks a tree-lined street. His team didn't even notice. His output improved.

Two years later, he's still CTO. The company's grown from 40 to 120 employees. He told me: "I didn't realize how much energy I was spending just existing in San Francisco until I stopped spending it."

From Map Pins to Meaning

A map doesn't tell you where to go. It only shows you what's possible.

The point of this book isn't to convince you to move. It's to help you design the version of Florida that fits you best.

There are executives here who live in quiet coastal towns, who work from home in shorts and run advisory calls from their back patio. Others split time between Miami and Manhattan, treating Florida as their base of operations. Some have built entire networks here that now anchor their companies, capital, and families.

What they all share is intentionality. They didn't stumble into this life; they engineered it.

That's what you'll learn to do in the pages ahead, to turn relocation from an idea into a system.

Action Plan: Your First Questions

Before you start looking at properties or calling moving companies, work through these exercises. They'll clarify whether this move makes strategic sense and what you're actually optimizing for.

1. Motivation Audit (15 minutes)

Exercise: Write down your top three motivations for considering Florida. Be specific. Not "better weather" but "I want to be outside more and I'm tired of 6-month winters affecting my mood."

For each motivation, answer:

- Is this a "moving away from" or "moving toward" driver?
- How will you measure whether this motivation is satisfied?

- What would need to be true for this to feel like a win?

Why this matters: Executives who move "toward" something (better lifestyle, network, ROI) succeed more often than those moving "away from" something (taxes, weather, burnout alone).

2. Friction Point Mapping (30 minutes)

Exercise: Create two columns. Label them "Energy Drains" and "What Adds Energy."

Spend 30 minutes listing every aspect of your current life:

- Your commute (or lack thereof)
- Your neighborhood
- Your tax situation
- Your daily routines
- Your network access
- Your family's satisfaction
- Your health and fitness patterns
- Your work environment

Be ruthlessly honest about what's actually working versus what you've learned to tolerate.

Success metric: If you have 3x more items in "Energy Drains" than "Adds Energy," relocation might be strategic.

3. Personal Burn Rate Calculator (1 hour)

Exercise: Calculate your monthly "personal burn rate". Not just housing and food, but everything:

- Housing costs (mortgage/rent, insurance, property tax, HOA, utilities)
- Transportation (car payments, insurance, gas, parking, maintenance)
- Taxes (federal, state, local - estimate monthly allocation)
- Healthcare (insurance premiums, typical out-of-pocket)

- Family costs (schools, childcare, activities)
- Lifestyle costs (dining, travel, entertainment, gym, subscriptions)

Then create a "Florida version" estimate using:

- Current Florida property costs in your target area
- Zero state income tax
- Estimated insurance costs (request quotes)
- Estimated lifestyle costs (research cost of living data)

Key insight: Most executives find their Florida burn rate is 20-35% lower, even with similar lifestyle quality.

4. Peer Interview Template (ongoing)

Exercise: Identify five peers or colleagues who have already relocated to Florida or similar markets. Schedule 30-minute calls with each.

Ask these five questions:

1. What surprised you most about the move (positive and negative)?
2. What do you wish you'd known before you started?
3. How long did it take before Florida felt like "home"?
4. What's different about your daily life now versus before?
5. If you were doing it again, what would you do differently?

Document their answers. Patterns will emerge that help you avoid common mistakes.

5. One-Year Vision Statement (30 minutes)

Exercise: Write one paragraph describing your ideal day, twelve months after a successful move to Florida. Be specific:

- What time do you wake up and why?
- What does your workspace look like?
- How does your workday flow?

- Who are you having dinner with?
- What does your evening or weekend look like?
- How do you feel when you go to bed?

Why this matters: This becomes your North Star. Every decision you make during relocation should move you closer to this vision, not away from it.

6. Decision Timeline (15 minutes)

Exercise: Answer these questions to clarify your timeline:

- Is this move happening in the next 6 months, 12 months, or 24+ months?
- What needs to happen before you can commit? (Job clarity, family agreement, financial milestone?)
- What would accelerate the timeline?
- What would cause you to postpone or cancel?

Be honest: If your answer is "someday when things slow down," this move probably won't happen. Someday needs a date.

YOUR RELOCATION ROI

THE NUMBERS BEHIND THE LIFESTYLE

EVERY EXECUTIVE HAS a mental spreadsheet running in the background. Even when you're not consciously looking at it, your brain is balancing inputs and outputs. Time spent versus value created. Stress taken versus satisfaction gained.

That same logic applies to where you live. The only difference is that most people never open the tab.

For years, I treated my cost of living as fixed. Taxes were just "what you paid for opportunity." Travel time was "the price of access." I could justify anything if the career upside was big enough. But at a certain point, the math stopped making sense.

It wasn't the salary that changed. It was the return.

Over my three decades in Florida, I've watched executives work through this calculation. The ones who relocate successfully don't just measure savings. They measure total return. They understand that ROI has two sides: the financial and the functional. The money you keep and the life you gain.

THE EXECUTIVE'S TIPPING POINT

You know that feeling when a project is profitable on paper but feels inefficient in practice? You look at the numbers and they add up, but something inside you says the model is off.

That's how relocation decisions begin for most senior leaders. You start realizing that the inputs of your current life; time, taxes, and tolerance, are no longer producing the same emotional or financial yield.

One friend, a Chief Product Officer at a public SaaS company, told me it hit him one night on a Zoom call at 8:45 p.m. He was still in the office. His kids had already gone to bed. The sun had set before he'd seen it.

He had done everything right by traditional standards. Big job, Bay Area house, equity package. Yet when he ran a simple thought experiment. What if I could do this job from anywhere? The answer changed everything.

He wasn't running away from Silicon Valley. He was simply re-evaluating the return.

Six months later, he was living in Seminole Heights (Tampa), had cut his personal burn rate by 30%, and told me his output had actually improved because he wasn't spending cognitive energy on logistics and overhead.

THE RELOCATION ROI EQUATION

Relocation ROI isn't just about saving money. It's about reclaiming leverage.

At its core, the equation looks like this:

FINANCIAL ROI + LIFESTYLE ROI = TOTAL RELOCATION ROI

Each side feeds the other. The financial gains give you freedom; the lifestyle gains give you endurance.

When both improve, you don't just make more. You last longer.

Let me break down both sides based on what I've seen work for executives over the past three decades.

Part 1: Financial ROI

The tangible side of relocation is easy to see. State income tax, property tax, cost of housing, flights instead of commutes. Most executives who move to Florida discover that the difference between "gross" and "net" feels like a raise without negotiation.

But the financial ROI isn't limited to what you keep. It's also what you unlock.

The Tax Component

Florida offers zero state income tax. No tax on wages, bonuses, stock options, or capital gains at the state level.

For a senior executive earning $400K+ in a high-tax state, the annual savings can range from $30K-$50K or more, depending on their original state. Over a decade, accounting for compensation growth, that compounds to $500K+ in savings.

But here's what most people miss: it's not just about your current salary. It's about liquidity events. The state tax difference on a significant equity event can represent hundreds of thousands in savings.

I've worked with CFOs and founders who've timed their Florida relocation specifically around major equity events. Done correctly, that's legitimate tax optimization that compounds significantly over a career.

The Cost of Living Reality

Florida isn't necessarily "cheap" anymore. Not in the markets where executives want to live. But it's dramatically more affordable than comparable coastal metros.

Tampa Bay housing (2024-2025): Quality single-family homes in desirable neighborhoods range from $550K-$850K. Comparable properties in San Francisco, Manhattan, or Boston run $1.5M-$2.5M+.

Even accounting for Florida's higher property insurance costs, the math works heavily in your favor. Monthly carry costs for a well-located Florida home run 40-50% less than equivalent housing in major coastal cities.

The Hidden Financial Multipliers

The financial ROI compounds in ways most people don't calculate:

Property appreciation: Florida real estate, particularly in Tampa Bay, has shown strong fundamentals over time. The region remains underpriced compared to other major metros.

Lower lifestyle costs: Dining, services, and general overhead typically run 20-30% less than major coastal cities.

Business efficiency: Florida's business-friendly environment often means lower costs for entities, licensing, and compliance.

Many executives find that proximity to capital and emerging markets more than replaces what they left behind. A founder I know who moved from Boston said it best, "The investors I used to chase now vacation where I live."

Part 2: Lifestyle ROI

The harder side to measure is how your energy compounds.

The first six months after moving, many executives report sleeping better, thinking clearer, and feeling a sense of forward motion they hadn't felt in years. It's not magic; it's margin.

When you remove friction, creativity comes back. You have time to walk in the morning, have dinner with family, or take an uninterrupted hour to plan instead of react. Those small improvements add up to better decisions and longer runways.

The biggest tax most executives pay isn't financial, it's cognitive. Every unnecessary stressor erodes focus. Lifestyle ROI gives that focus back.

Time Reclamation

In my three decades here, I've watched executives reclaim time in ways that surprise them:

Commute elimination: Even a 45-minute each-way commute represents nearly 10 full work weeks per year. That's time returned to strategic thinking, family, or rest.

Weather access: 300+ sunny days means outdoor activity becomes routine. Morning walks, weekend resets, evening exercise. These aren't luxuries here. They're lifestyle patterns that compound into better health and performance.

Travel efficiency: Tampa International and other Florida airports offer excellent connectivity to business hubs nationwide, often with easier logistics and lower costs than from congested metros.

Family integration: When outdoor access is year-round, when family time doesn't compete with logistics, quality of life improves measurably.

Energy Economics

Here's something I've observed over the past couple decades: executives operate on energy budgets, not just time budgets.

You have a finite amount of decision-making energy each day. When you spend it on traffic, weather frustration, tax complexity, and logistical friction, there's less left for strategy, creativity, and leadership.

Florida's environment: the weather, the pace, the lower overhead - preserves energy. You wake up with more capacity. You end the day with reserves left.

That might sound soft, but it shows up in hard outcomes: better decisions, more patience with your team, creative problem-solving instead of reactive firefighting.

One CTO told me: "I didn't realize I'd been operating on 70% capacity until I moved here and discovered what 90% felt like."

Network Quality Over Quantity

Here's a nuanced point about lifestyle ROI: Florida's executive community is smaller than Silicon Valley or New York, but the signal-to-noise ratio is better.

In San Francisco, you could attend three networking events every night. In Tampa Bay, there are fewer events, but the people at them are more likely to be serious operators building real things.

Relationships form faster here because there's less performative networking and more genuine connection. That shift from quantity to quality is hard to measure in spreadsheets, but it shows up in the deals that get done and the friendships that stick.

Part 3: The Compounding Effect

The most interesting thing about ROI is how it compounds over time.

The first year, you notice the financial savings: the larger paychecks, the lower overhead. The second year, you notice the health improvements: better sleep, more energy, consistent exercise. By year three, you notice it in your patience, creativity, and decision quality.

That's when you realize relocation isn't a reward for success. It's an enabler of future success.

The executives who thrive post-move are the ones who track both sides of the equation. They build a simple dashboard, not complex, just visible. Because what gets measured gets optimized.

SEEING ROI BEYOND THE NUMBERS

Not all returns are financial.

Some of the highest-yield outcomes I've seen from executives who relocated had nothing to do with cash. One regained time with aging parents. Another started mentoring startups again because he finally had bandwidth. A third finally launched the nonprofit he'd been dreaming about since his Series C exit.

They all said the same thing: "I didn't realize how small my world had become until I made it bigger."

That's the true payoff of relocation: the expansion of possibility.

THE HIDDEN COSTS OF STAYING STILL

Every investment has an opportunity cost. Staying where you are is no exception.

Executives often underestimate how much the environment shapes decision quality. If your daily inputs are chaos and congestion, your decisions eventually reflect that.

Florida won't automatically fix poor thinking. But proximity to calm creates space for better thinking.

In high-performing environments, we talk about "burn rate" in financial terms. I like to ask about *personal burn rate.* How much energy are you spending to sustain your current success? How much longer is that sustainable?

When your personal burn rate exceeds your professional growth rate, the curve eventually breaks.

That's why thinking about relocation through an ROI lens matters. It reframes the move from emotional to operational.

DESIGNING YOUR ROI DASHBOARD

Before you pack a single box, start by designing your own version of an ROI dashboard.

Ask yourself:

- What measurable returns would make this move worthwhile?
- What qualitative returns would make it meaningful?

You might list financial markers: lower taxes, reduced overhead, property appreciation. Then add personal markers: energy, family time, creative flow.

When you look at both sets side by side, you'll see where the real value lies.

One executive I coached created a simple "Life P&L." On the left were costs: taxes, rent, commute, time away from family. On the right were gains: focus, access to sunshine, personal bandwidth.

He didn't need to run a complex model. He could see the imbalance instantly.

MAKING ROI PERSONAL

Here's how to think about ROI in a way that fits your life stage:

If you're still building: Relocation ROI might look like extending your runway. Lower overhead, more time, better focus.

If you're scaling: It might be about reach. New markets, new investors, new lifestyle credibility.

If you're transitioning: It might be about sustainability. Protecting what you've built while gaining the freedom to enjoy it.

Each version is valid. The only mistake is assuming ROI is the same for everyone.

Your formula should fit your priorities, not someone else's narrative.

The Takeaway

Relocation isn't about leaving something behind. It's about investing in what's next.

When you treat your move like an ROI exercise, you give it structure. You create accountability. You make sure the life you're building in Florida pays you back in more than money.

That's how professionals move with intention. They don't just ask, "Can I afford it?" They ask, "Does it return value?"

ACTION PLAN: BUILDING YOUR RELOCATION ROI

1. Define Your Personal ROI

Write your own definition of *return*: What would make the move worthwhile beyond finances? Include both financial and lifestyle metrics that matter to you.

2. List Expected Improvements

Create two columns: three financial improvements you expect from relocating and three lifestyle improvements. Be specific and measurable where possible.

3. Calculate Your Current Cost

Track your "personal burn rate" for one month. Note what drains your energy (commute, logistics, stress) and what restores it (family time, rest, creative work).

4. Create Your Life P&L

On one side, list the costs of staying (financial, time, energy). On the other, list the gains of moving (savings, freedom, quality of life). Let the comparison speak for itself.

5. Identify Your Success Metric

Choose one metric you'll revisit six months after moving to measure progress. Examples: energy level (1-10), hours with family per week, creative projects started, or sleep quality.

6. Share and Validate

Share your draft ROI framework with a peer who's already relocated. Ask for feedback on what surprised them and what they wish they'd tracked from day one.

BECOME A FLORIDIAN (DOMICILE PROOF STACK)

BUILDING YOUR PAPER TRAIL

RELOCATION DOESN'T BECOME REAL the day the moving truck pulls away. It becomes real the day the state you left stops claiming you.

Many executives don't realize this until months later, when a letter arrives from their former state asking why they still owe taxes. They thought they moved. The state thought they didn't.

That gap between perception and proof is where domicile lives.

In all my years in Florida, I've watched this play out hundreds of times. Brilliant executives who optimize everything in their business life treat domicile like an afterthought, until it becomes expensive. The difference between "I moved to Florida" and "I can prove I'm a Florida resident" is worth more than most real estate commissions.

WHY DOMICILE MATTERS

Domicile is the legal term for where your life officially resides. It isn't just an address. It's where the state believes your *intent* lies. You can own homes in several places, but you can have only one domicile.

For executives, that distinction matters more than ever. It affects how your bonuses, stock options, capital gains, and estate are treated. It decides whether a tax authority considers your relocation valid or reversible.

In plain terms, domicile is the paper trail of your intent. It tells the story of where you belong.

And here's something I've learned from working with C-level executives who've gone through audits: states like New York, California, and New Jersey have dedicated residency audit teams. They're sophisticated, well-funded, and they know exactly what to look for.

They're not auditing you because they think you're dishonest. They're auditing you because you're worth auditing. High earners are high-value targets.

THE ILLUSION OF MOVING

A lot of people assume domicile changes automatically when they move. They sell their house, buy a new one, and update their LinkedIn location. But that's not how the system works.

Old states don't let go easily, especially ones that rely heavily on income tax. New York, California, New Jersey. These places have teams whose entire job is to challenge relocation claims.

I've watched executives lose six figures to audits because they didn't document their transition properly. They assumed the lifestyle was enough proof. It wasn't.

The technical reality is this: domicile is determined by a combination of objective facts (where you live, work, bank, vote, register your car) and subjective intent (where you consider "home"). When those two don't align clearly, states can and do challenge your claim.

THE CAUTIONARY TALE OF MARK

Mark was a senior VP at a fintech firm in Manhattan. When remote work became permanent, he bought a condo in Miami and started splitting his time. His family stayed in New York for the school year, but he spent most weeks in Florida.

He changed his driver's license, registered to vote, even joined a local gym. But he didn't sell the New York home. He didn't move his primary bank accounts. And his accountant kept mailing everything to his Manhattan address.

Two years later, New York audited him. The state determined he was still a resident because his "center of gravity" remained in Manhattan. The audit cost him more than any tax savings he'd thought he'd earned.

Mark hadn't done anything dishonest. He'd simply left the story half-told.

When I work with executives now, I share Mark's story early. Not to scare them, but to show them that domicile is a system, not a checkbox. You can't do it halfway.

THE DOMICILE PROOF STACK

To avoid stories like Mark's, you need a framework. A way to build irrefutable evidence of your new life. I call it the **Domicile Proof Stack.**

Think of it as layers of credibility that reinforce one another. Each layer tells part of the story, but together they create a complete picture that can withstand scrutiny.

After three decades of watching relocations succeed and fail, I've seen this framework work consistently:

Layer 1: Intent

This is the foundation. You have to *decide* that Florida is home, and your actions must reflect that decision consistently.

Intent shows up in the documents you sign and the statements you make. It's visible in filing a Florida Declaration of Domicile, moving your entire household, joining local organizations, and changing your professional address on all business documents.

Intent is the narrative thread that ties everything together. Without it, the rest of the stack falls apart.

Here's how I explain intent to executives: if someone looked at your life from the outside - your calendar, your bank statements, your mail, your social connections. Would they conclude you live in Florida or are you just visiting?

Layer 2: Paperwork

Next comes the tangible layer: the records that formalize your intent.

This is the bureaucratic infrastructure of domicile, and it's non-negotiable. The essentials include:

Immediate actions (within 30 days): Florida driver's license, vehicle registration, voter registration, and Declaration of Domicile filed with the county clerk.

Early follow-up (within 90 days): Update mailing addresses with USPS, banks, the IRS, and all insurance policies. Change addresses with your employer and professional licenses.

Mid-term updates (within 6 months): Update estate planning documents to reflect Florida law, move primary banking relationships, and change addresses on business entities.

These are the signals auditors look for first. They want to see whether your legal and financial life matches your claim of residency.

Layer 3: Presence

Intent and paperwork mean little if you aren't physically here.

Florida doesn't require a minimum number of days like some states, but the states you leave often do. New York, for example, uses a "183-

day rule". If you spend 183 days or more in New York, you're presumed to be a resident.

But even beyond state-specific rules, presence proves commitment. Track your physical location through calendar entries, flight confirmations, utility bills, credit card statements, and cell phone data.

I tell executives: think like an auditor. If someone challenged your residency, could you prove where you were on any given day?

The Family Factor:

If your spouse and children remain in your old state while you're in Florida, that complicates the domicile picture significantly. Auditors view this as evidence that your "home" is still where your family is.

If you must split time initially, document it carefully: show that it's temporary with a specific end date, keep proof of your intent to reunify the family in Florida, and don't maintain a permanent residence in the old state during this transition.

Layer 4: Patterns

Finally, the top of the stack: your habits.

This is the human layer: where you spend weekends, where your doctor is, where your family gathers for holidays, where your kids go to school, where you worship, where you volunteer.

These are the details that give your story credibility. Auditors often call this "lifestyle evidence." When your daily patterns reflect Florida life, no spreadsheet can argue otherwise.

What this looks like in practice: primary care physician in Florida, dentist in Florida, gym membership, club or community memberships, kids enrolled in Florida schools, charitable giving to Florida organizations, banking relationships with Florida-based institutions.

Together, these four layers; Intent, Paperwork, Presence, and Patterns, form the **Domicile Proof Stack.** Build it deliberately, and you'll never have to prove it defensively.

THE STORY OF CARLA

Let me show you what this looks like when done right.

Carla was a Chief Operating Officer for a healthcare startup in Boston. She planned her relocation like a merger; systematically and completely.

Before moving, she created a checklist of every official connection to Massachusetts: voting registration, car titles, family trusts, mailing addresses, professional memberships, medical providers, bank accounts, everything. She and her attorney mapped out what needed to migrate and when.

When she moved, she did it completely. Her family came with her. She registered in Florida, joined a local nonprofit board, and started hosting her team offsites in Tampa instead of Cambridge.

Two years later, Massachusetts audited her. The state claimed she was still a resident.

Carla's attorney submitted a binder of documentation that told the opposite story: Florida driver's license, utility bills showing continuous occupancy, travel logs proving she spent 280+ days in Florida, club memberships, even her kids' school enrollment and medical records.

The audit ended quickly. The case closed in her favor.

Carla didn't just move; she executed. And that execution was worth hundreds of thousands of dollars in tax certainty.

When I tell this story to new clients, the lesson is always the same: domicile is a project, not a formality. Treat it like you would a product launch, with clear milestones, accountability, and verification.

WHAT SMART EXECUTIVES DO DIFFERENTLY

Executives who handle domicile correctly treat it as a project, not a formality. They create timelines, assign responsibilities, and verify completion.

A good rule of thumb: if it's significant enough to affect your taxes, investments, or identity, it needs to be updated.

Smart movers also coordinate across advisors; legal, financial, and tax. Many mistakes happen because each professional assumes someone else handled it.

You wouldn't roll out a new product without QA testing. Treat your domicile the same way.

Create a Domicile Coordination Team with your CPA, attorney, real estate advisor, and financial advisor. Hold one coordination call before you move to align everyone on the timeline and responsibilities. Then hold follow-up calls at 30, 90, and 180 days to verify completion.

This level of coordination might seem excessive, but I've watched it save executives from expensive mistakes repeatedly.

WHEN INTENT AND REALITY CONFLICT

Sometimes, intent and reality clash. Maybe you moved first and your family follows later. Maybe you still travel back monthly for board meetings. Maybe your company keeps a mailing address in your old city.

These aren't dealbreakers, but they need explanation. The key is to document the transition. Keep a record of your timeline. Show that your move is deliberate, not temporary.

The state doesn't expect perfection. It expects consistency.

The pattern I've seen since the 90s: the cleaner and more complete your transition, the less likely you'll face challenges later.

THE EMOTIONAL SIDE OF PROOF

There's also a personal dimension to this process. Domicile is about identity as much as paperwork.

When I moved to Florida in the 90s, there was a moment when it clicked. It wasn't when I changed my driver's license or registered to vote. It was when I caught myself saying "back home" and meaning here.

That shift. When your heart and your paperwork finally agree. Is what makes you a Floridian.

The legal side matters because it protects you. The emotional side matters because it grounds you. Together they form confidence that the move was more than geography.

HOW TO THINK LIKE AN AUDITOR

To see how your Proof Stack holds up, reverse the perspective. Imagine you're the auditor.

What story would your current records tell?

If someone reviewed your accounts, travel logs, medical records, and professional addresses, would they see a clear move or a mixed message?

I recommend running this test once a year, especially in your first three years as a Florida resident, which are the highest audit risk period.

Here's a simple audit simulation exercise: Print your last 12 months of credit card statements (what percentage of charges are in Florida?), review your calendar (how many days in Florida vs. elsewhere?), look at your mail (does everything come to Florida?), check your professional profiles (do they all show Florida?), and review your medical records (when was your last appointment with a Florida-based doctor?).

If you find gaps or inconsistencies, fix them immediately. Don't wait for an audit.

THE COMMON MISTAKES

After years of watching relocations, I can tell you the five mistakes that cause the most problems:

Mistake 1: Leaving Financial Accounts Untouched - If your main bank, brokerage, or accountant is still in your old state, that weakens your case. Open primary banking relationships in Florida.

Mistake 2: Keeping a "Primary" Home Elsewhere - Owning property in multiple states is fine, but your Florida home should be your nicest, largest, or most valuable property.

Mistake 3: Filing Taxes Inconsistently - Work with a CPA who specializes in multi-state relocations. File your part-year return properly the year you move.

Mistake 4: Ignoring Family Logistics - If family must stay temporarily, document the plan for reunification clearly with a specific end date.

Mistake 5: Relying on Assumptions - Work with professionals who specialize in executive relocations. The cost of proper guidance is tiny compared to the cost of an audit.

Every one of these mistakes stems from treating the move casually instead of systematically.

Why Your Real Estate Advisor Should Understand Domicile

Your home purchase is one of the most important domicile documents you'll create. How you structure it, when you close it, and how you use it all become part of your paper trail.

When selecting a real estate advisor, look for someone who understands domicile requirements and can coordinate with your CPA and attorney on timing, ownership structure, and documentation. The purchase timing should support your domicile timeline, the property type and size should send the right signals about permanence, the ownership structure should align with your estate plan, and the closing date shouldn't conflict with your tax year strategy.

THE CONFIDENCE DIVIDEND

Once your Proof Stack is complete, something subtle but powerful happens. You stop worrying about what could go wrong and start focusing on what can grow.

You can sell equity, take liquidity events, and plan estate moves without hesitation. You can enjoy the lifestyle benefits of Florida without looking over your shoulder.

Confidence becomes its own ROI.

I've seen this transformation hundreds of times over the years. Executives who initially felt anxious about their domicile status eventually relax into certainty. That psychological shift from "I hope this works" to "I know this is solid" affects everything else.

That's what a proper Domicile Proof Stack buys you: freedom from worry.

ACTION PLAN: BUILDING YOUR DOMICILE PROOF STACK

1. Write Your Intent Statement

Create a one-paragraph statement describing why Florida is now your permanent home. Date it, sign it, and keep it with your relocation records. This becomes part of your paper trail.

2. Create Your Master Checklist

List every document, account, or registration that still reflects your old address. Include banks, credit cards, licenses, memberships, medical providers, and professional affiliations. Schedule updates over the next 30 days.

3. Track Your Physical Presence

Set up a system to document where you are each day for your first full year. Use calendar entries, travel confirmations, or a simple spreadsheet. This becomes your audit defense.

4. Establish Florida Patterns

Move at least three major professional or personal relationships to Florida within 90 days: find a Florida banker, doctor, or community role. Join one organization and attend one event per month.

5. Conduct a Self-Audit

Ask yourself: "If a tax authority reviewed my life today, would my story be clear?" Review credit card statements, calendar, mail, and professional profiles. Fix any gaps immediately.

6. Celebrate the Moment

Mark the moment you catch yourself saying "back home" and meaning Florida. That's when you've truly arrived.

THE TIMING TRIAD

YOUR MIGRATION RELEASE SCHEDULE

WHEN PEOPLE TALK ABOUT RELOCATION, they usually focus on location. When executives talk about relocation, they focus on timing.

Timing, more than any other variable, decides whether a move feels like liberation or regret. The difference between a smart transition and an expensive one is often measured in weeks, not years.

You don't have to be a finance professional to understand this; you live it every year. There's a cadence to executive life; performance reviews, vesting schedules, annual bonuses, equity cliffs. Each of those cycles runs on a calendar that rarely matches your personal one.

The smartest movers learn to align the two. They treat timing as an asset, not an afterthought.

In my time working with executives who've relocated to Florida, I've seen timing make or break relocations more than any other factor. Two executives with identical financial situations can have dramatically different outcomes based purely on when they execute their move.

THE CALENDAR YOU DIDN'T KNOW YOU WERE MANAGING

Every executive has at least three calendars running in parallel. They just rarely put them on the same page.

1. The Personal Calendar

This one feels obvious: when school years begin and end, when leases expire, when family can handle a move. It's the human side of timing, and it's usually the one that forces the decision. But it's also the least negotiable.

You can't tell your kids "We're moving in March instead of June because of tax optimization." Well, you can, but you'll pay for it in family stress.

2. The Financial Calendar

This is where most mistakes happen. Bonuses, vesting cliffs, profit sharing, carried interest, and liquidity events all follow specific time-lines. If your move crosses one of them, the tax treatment of your income can change dramatically.

This is the calendar that executives often underestimate. They focus on the house and the logistics but forget that a three-month timing difference could mean $50K-$100K in tax implications.

3. The Legal Calendar

States measure residency by tax year. That means when and where you are on December 31st can matter as much as what you earn. Understanding the cutoff points between tax years, and which state you were domiciled in when key events occurred, can save you significant friction later.

Together, these three make up what I call **The Timing Triad**: the synchronization of your **Personal** life, **Financial** life, and **Legal** life around a single move.

WHY TIMING MATTERS MORE THAN LUCK

I once knew a VP of Engineering who joked that his last "bad year" cost him more than his first car.

He had sold stock options in March, moved in June, and filed in April of the following year. In his head, the order made sense. On paper, it created a tax headache because he technically realized income while still domiciled in his old state.

He wasn't careless. He was just focused on everything else a move requires: schools, movers, leases, team transitions. By the time he thought about the financial sequence, it was already too late.

For most of us, that story sounds familiar. We've all missed opportunities not because we lacked information, but because we handled the right details in the wrong order.

Timing is leverage. When you manage it intentionally, the same actions yield better results.

Over three decades in Florida, I've helped executives avoid this trap by treating timing like a product launch: with planning, sequencing, and clear milestones. The ones who succeed don't just move. They orchestrate.

THE PERSONAL CALENDAR

This is where your move begins, because life has its own logic. No spreadsheet can account for school enrollment, family readiness, or personal bandwidth. You can't just relocate an executive; you relocate a household.

The most effective movers I know treat this like a series of sprints, not a marathon. They stage decisions: first, get clarity with family; second, line up housing and schools; third, communicate to their companies.

By sequencing personal milestones first, you prevent emotional friction later. It's hard to optimize taxes when you're still negotiating bedtime routines across time zones.

THE KEY QUESTIONS FOR YOUR PERSONAL CALENDAR:

- **School timing:** If you have kids, when does it make sense to transition them? Mid-year is possible but harder. Summer is cleaner.
- **Family readiness:** Is everyone on board? If not, what needs to happen first? Forced moves create resentment.
- **Housing logistics:** Do you need to sell before you buy? Can you overlap for a transition period? What's your cash flow situation?
- **Work flexibility:** Can you go fully remote immediately, or do you need a transition period? Does your company support this?
- **Life events:** Any major events (weddings, graduations, health issues) that would make relocation harder in certain windows?

The key to the personal calendar is momentum. Make one firm decision, usually the school year or home closing, and let everything else orbit around that. Once your family rhythm locks in, you can focus on aligning money and legal details to match it.

THE FINANCIAL CALENDAR

The financial side of timing is less visible but more powerful. Every executive has a compensation structure tied to specific dates:

- Base pay cycles
- Annual bonuses
- Vesting cliffs for restricted stock or options
- Performance grants
- Deferred compensation schedules
- Profit sharing distributions
- Carried interest payments

The question isn't whether those events happen; it's where you live when they do.

A few months' difference can determine how your earnings are sourced for tax purposes. That's why timing the financial calendar around your move is so critical.

THE TAX YEAR REALITY

Here's what most executives don't fully grasp until they're in the middle of it:

States measure residency by tax year (January 1 to December 31). If you move in the middle of a tax year, you'll file as a "part-year resident" in both states.

What that means:

- Income earned while domiciled in your old state = taxed by old state
- Income earned while domiciled in Florida = no state tax
- The burden is on you to prove when the domicile change occurred

This is why timing matters so much. If you have a $200K bonus that vests in February, and you moved in March, your old state will likely claim that bonus was "earned" during the prior year when you were still a resident, even though you received it after moving.

ILLUSTRATIVE SCENARIO: THE CALENDAR MISALIGNMENT

Let me show you how timing can create expensive complications:

Meet Lisa, a senior executive at a public SaaS company. Her compensation structure:

- $350K base salary
- $150K annual bonus (paid in February)
- RSUs that vest quarterly

She planned her Florida move for early March 2024, thinking: "I'll get my bonus, then move. Clean and simple."

The problem: Her bonus was earned over the 2023 calendar year when she was a Massachusetts resident. Even though she received it in February 2024 after deciding to move, Massachusetts still considered it taxable income because:

1. It was earned during her Massachusetts residency period
2. She was still technically a Massachusetts resident when paid (hadn't established Florida domicile yet)

The tax hit: ~$20K in Massachusetts state tax on that bonus.

What if she'd timed it differently?

Alternative timeline:

- November 2023: Make the decision to move
- December 2023: Move to Florida, establish domicile before year-end
- January 2024: File declaration of domicile, get Florida driver's license
- February 2024: Receive bonus as a Florida resident
- Result: $0 state tax on the bonus

The six-week timing difference between "move in March" and "move in December" cost her $20K.

Now multiply that by a career of equity vests, bonuses, and liquidity events. Small timing decisions create big outcome differences.

This example isn't about taxes (I'm not a CPA), it's about awareness. The order of operations matters.

THE LEGAL CALENDAR

States run on calendar years. They think in 12-month blocks, not in the fluid way executives live and work.

That creates friction. You can start working in Florida in May and still owe partial-year taxes elsewhere. You can move in October and still be seen as a resident of your old state for that tax year if you haven't properly established domicile.

Understanding how those systems measure time gives you control. It's the difference between being classified as a "part-year resident" (complex) and being seen as fully transitioned (clean).

KEY LEGAL CALENDAR CONCEPTS:

The December 31st Line

For tax purposes, your domicile on December 31st matters enormously. If you establish Florida domicile before year-end, you start the new year clean. If you wait until January, you're creating a part-year situation.

This is why I often recommend executives who are serious about moving to do it in Q4 rather than waiting for the "perfect" time in Q1 or Q2.

Q4 move advantages:

- Clean break at year-end
- Next year's compensation is fully Florida-based
- Holiday season gives family transition time
- Less disruption to school year (if you time it for winter break)

Q1 move challenges:

- Part-year resident filing in two states
- Bonus timing complications
- Have to live with complexity for 12+ months

THE 183-DAY RULE (FOR SOME STATES)

Some states (particularly New York) use a "statutory residency" test: if you maintain a permanent place of abode in the state AND spend 183+ days there, you're presumed to be a resident regardless of your "domicile."

This creates a gotcha for executives who move to Florida but still have a home in their old state and travel back frequently.

Example: You move to Florida, establish domicile, but keep a pied-à-terre in Manhattan. If you spend 184 days in New York (even as short visits that add up), New York could claim you as a statutory resident and tax all your income.

Solution: If you're keeping property in your old state, track your days meticulously. Stay under 183 days. Better yet, don't keep a residence there at all.

HOW THE TRIAD INTERACTS

These three calendars don't operate independently; they overlap. If you align them, you create a smooth transition. If you don't, they compete for attention.

Imagine trying to finalize a house purchase while your equity is vesting, your family is still in another state, and your tax domicile hasn't changed yet. You end up managing chaos instead of executing a plan.

The Triad simplifies that. Start with your **personal calendar**: the non-negotiables of family and life. Overlay your **financial calendar**: where money events occur. Then sync your **legal calendar**: how the state will interpret those dates.

When those align, the rest of the process feels almost frictionless.

Example of good alignment:

Personal: Kids finish school year in June, family ready to move in July

Financial: Annual bonus paid in February (before move), next equity vest in October (after move and domicile establishment)

Legal: Establish Florida domicile in July/August, well before next tax year

Result: Clean transition. Bonus already received and taxed (no complexity). Family moves together during summer. Domicile established before next compensation events. Next year files as full Florida resident.

Example of poor alignment:

Personal: Family moves in March (mid-school year, high stress)

Financial: Equity vests in April (one month after move, before domicile is solid)

Legal: Part-year resident filing required, domicile timing questioned by old state

Result: Family stress, tax complexity, potential audit risk, suboptimal timing of major financial event.

The difference between these scenarios isn't luck, it's planning.

SUCCESS STORY: SARAH'S ORCHESTRATED MOVE

Let me show you what this looks like when done well.

Sarah was a Chief Revenue Officer for a cybersecurity firm in New York. Her company was planning an IPO within 12 months, and she knew her equity value would increase substantially.

She wanted to establish Florida domicile before the IPO to avoid New York state tax on her eventual stock sales. But she also needed to consider her family (two kids in school) and her professional obligations (still running revenue for the company).

Her Timing Triad analysis:

Personal Calendar:

- School year ends mid-June
- Didn't want to disrupt kids mid-year
- Husband could work remotely from anywhere
- Target move window: July / August

Financial Calendar:

- Annual bonus paid in March
- IPO expected in October
- Lockup expires 180 days post-IPO (April next year)
- Next equity vest: quarterly, so one in September
- Critical goal: Be Florida resident before IPO

Legal Calendar:

- Needed to establish domicile before October IPO
- Wanted to avoid part-year resident complexity
- Preferred to establish domicile in Q3 to have clear full-year filing next year

Her timeline:

March: Received annual bonus as NY resident (no way to avoid this, already earned)

April-May: House hunting trips to Tampa Bay, selected South Tampa neighborhood

June: Kids finished school, family sold NY home

July:

- Moved to Florida
- Filed Declaration of Domicile immediately
- Got Florida driver's license, voter registration

- Kids enrolled in new schools for fall

August:

- Established banking relationships, medical providers
- Joined local business groups
- Started hosting investor meetings in Tampa

October: Company IPO occurred. Sarah was clearly a Florida resident.

April (next year): Lockup expired, Sarah sold portion of stock. Zero state tax on gains.

Result: Sarah saved approximately $250K in state taxes on her initial post-lockup sale. Over the following years, as she sold more stock, the savings compounded into seven figures.

But beyond the money, she told me the timing alignment gave her peace of mind. She wasn't worried about audits, part-year complications, or whether she'd "done it right." She knew she had.

The orchestration took 6 months of planning but decades of value.

When I work with executives, this is what I mean by treating timing as leverage. Sarah didn't rush. She didn't delay. She synchronized three calendars around a clear goal and executed systematically.

MOMENTUM VERSUS RUSH

Many executives confuse momentum with speed. The point of planning isn't to move faster; it's to move cleaner.

When you line up your calendars, everything feels like a controlled rollout. When you skip the planning, it feels like a scramble.

The difference is attention.

Moving is already emotional. Adding chaos to the financial and legal side turns it into a burden. Timing creates calm.

In my experience helping executives relocate, the pattern is clear: the people who take 3-6 months to plan their timing execute in weeks. The people who "just do it" spend years cleaning up complexity.

How to Rehearse the Move

Treat your relocation like a product launch. Here's the process I use with executives:

Step 1: Pick Your Target Date

Start with your personal calendar. When does your family need this to happen?

If you have kids: summer is almost always better than mid-year.

If you don't: consider Q4 for tax simplicity.

Step 2: Work Backward

From your target date, map backward:

- 3 months before: house hunting, school selection
- 2 months before: finalize purchase, pack
- 1 month before: coordinate with employer, notify networks
- Move date: execute
- Immediately after: domicile establishment sprint

Step 3: Plot Major Milestones

On a single timeline (I like a large whiteboard or digital project manager), plot:

- Personal: family events, school calendar, lease dates
- Financial: bonus dates, equity vests, any liquidity events
- Legal: tax year boundaries, domicile deadlines

Look for conflicts. Are you trying to close on a house the same week your equity vests? Are you establishing domicile during your busiest quarter?

Step 4: Identify and Resolve Conflicts

If you see timing conflicts, adjust.

Can you delay the move by 6 weeks to get past a major equity event?

Can you accelerate to get domicile established before year-end?

Can you stage the move (you first, family follows 2 months later)?

Step 5: Create Your Master Timeline

Build a single document that shows:

- Week-by-week view of the 3 months before and after move date
- Key milestones with owners assigned
- Financial events highlighted in one color
- Legal deadlines highlighted in another
- Personal events in a third

Share this with your advisory team (CPA, attorney, real estate advisor) and get their input.

Step 6: Execute With Checkpoints

Don't just create the plan and hope. Build in checkpoints:

- 90 days out: confirm plan still works
- 60 days out: confirm all parties aligned
- 30 days out: final coordination
- Move day: execute
- 30 days after: verify domicile stack complete
- 90 days after: review with CPA, confirm tax strategy on track

Doing this exercise doesn't just save money; it gives you confidence. You can explain your decision to anyone; auditors, family, investors, because the story makes sense.

THE "PEACE OF MIND" DIVIDEND

Executives who move with timing awareness often describe something intangible afterward. They say the move felt easier, that decisions came faster, that their energy wasn't wasted on cleanup.

That's the hidden ROI of the Timing Triad. It isn't only financial; it's psychological. You stop second-guessing yourself. You stop wondering if you moved at the wrong time.

When your calendars align, so does your focus.

I've seen this hundreds of times: executives who plan their timing sleep better, work better, and build their Florida life faster because they're not carrying anxiety about "did I do this right?"

That confidence is priceless.

WHY YOUR REAL ESTATE ADVISOR SHOULD UNDERSTAND YOUR CALENDAR

When timing your property purchase, coordinate with your real estate advisor to ensure the closing aligns with your equity vesting schedule, bonus timing, and domicile establishment needs. The purchase should support your overall timing strategy, not complicate it.

For example, if you need to establish domicile before a major equity event in October, your property closing should happen no later than August or early September, giving you time to move in, establish presence, and complete your domicile documentation before the critical date.

Action Plan: Applying the Timing Triad

Work through these exercises to build your optimal relocation timeline:

1. Draw Your Master Timeline (2 hours)

Create a visual timeline showing the next 18 months with three parallel tracks:

Track 1 - Personal:

- School calendar (if applicable)
- Family events (graduations, weddings, etc.)
- Lease expiration dates
- Current housing situation

Track 2 - Financial:

- Base pay schedule
- Bonus payment dates
- Equity vesting schedule (all dates for next 18 months)
- Any planned liquidity events
- Deferred compensation elections or distributions

Track 3 - Legal:

- Current tax year boundary (December 31)
- Ideal domicile establishment date
- Part-year filing implications
- Any state-specific thresholds (183-day rules, etc.)

Tool suggestions:

- Large whiteboard or poster paper
- Digital project management tool (Asana, Notion, Monday)
- Excel with Gantt chart view
- Or just three parallel rows in a document

Success metric: You can see all three calendars at once and identify where they conflict or align.

2. Identify Your Critical Milestones (30 minutes)

On your master timeline, circle or highlight the 5-8 events that cannot move:

Examples:

- School year end date
- Major equity vest
- Annual bonus payment
- Current lease expiration
- Tax year boundary

These become your fixed points. Everything else flexes around them.

3. Find Your Optimal Move Window (45 minutes)

Based on your critical milestones, identify your ideal move window.

Ask:

- When can my family actually relocate without major disruption?
- When do I need to be domiciled in Florida to optimize my next financial event?
- What's the cleanest tax year timing?

Most executives find their optimal window is either:

- **Summer (June-August):** Good for families with school-age kids
- **Q4 (October-December):** Good for tax year simplicity

Write down your target date range.

4. Map Your Compensation Events (1 hour)

Get out your compensation documents and create a calendar of every payment date for the next 24 months:

- When is base salary paid? (typically doesn't matter, but good to know)
- When are bonuses paid? (critical)
- When do equity grants vest? (critical)

- When do stock options expire?
- When are profit sharing or carried interest distributions?
- Any other compensation events?

For each one, note:

- Date
- Approximate value
- Estimated state tax if received in old state vs. Florida

Success metric: You know exactly how much is at stake for different timing decisions.

5. Sequence Your Domicile Establishment (30 minutes)

Based on your optimal move window, create a day-by-day plan for your first 30 days in Florida:

Day 1-7: Move, unpack essentials, establish residence

Day 8-14: File Declaration of Domicile, get driver's license, register to vote

Day 15-21: Register vehicles, open Florida bank account

Day 22-30: Update all addresses, notify employer, establish local services

Why this matters: The faster you complete your domicile stack, the less exposure you have to timing complications.

6. Risk Assessment Matrix (45 minutes)

For your proposed move date, assess timing risks:

If you move earlier than planned:

- What gets harder? (family readiness, housing availability)
- What gets better? (tax optimization, domicile clarity)
- What's the cost/benefit?

If you move later than planned:

- What gets harder? (potential tax complications, missed financial events)
- What gets better? (more time to prepare, less rush)
- What's the cost/benefit?

If you split the timing (you move first, family follows):

- What are the domicile implications?
- What's the family stress level?
- Is this even feasible given your situation?

This risk assessment helps you decide if your current timing plan is truly optimal or needs adjustment.

7. Coordinate With Your Advisory Team (1-2 hours total)

Schedule coordination calls with your key advisors:

Call 1 - Your CPA (45 minutes):

- Share your proposed move timeline
- Ask: "Given my compensation structure, does this timing optimize my tax situation?"
- Discuss: part-year filing implications, domicile requirements
- Get: specific action items and deadlines

Call 2 - Your Attorney (45 minutes):

- Share your proposed timeline
- Ask: "Are there any legal or entity structure implications I'm missing?"
- Discuss: estate document updates, trust relocations, entity registrations
- Get: checklist of legal tasks with timing

Call 3 - Your Real Estate Advisor (45 minutes):

- Share your full Timing Triad analysis
- Ask: "How does this timing align with the Florida real estate market?"
- Discuss: house hunting timeline, closing coordination, market conditions
- Get: property search and closing timeline that fits your dates

Success metric: All three advisors are aligned on your timeline and understand how their work intersects.

8. Build Your Countdown Plan (1 hour)

From your target move date, create a week-by-week countdown:

12 weeks out:

- Finalize Florida neighborhood selection
- Start house hunting (virtual and in-person trips)
- Notify employer of plans

10 weeks out:

- Make offer on property
- Coordinate closing date with move date
- Research schools (if applicable)

8 weeks out:

- Finalize purchase contract
- Schedule movers
- Start packing non-essentials

6 weeks out:

- Coordinate with advisors on domicile plan

- Begin address update process
- Notify kids' current school

4 weeks out:

- Final coordination with all parties
- Complete most packing
- Confirm all logistics

2 weeks out:

- Final walkthrough of new property
- Confirm moving day details
- Travel to Florida for closing if needed

Move week:

- Close on property
- Move day
- Begin domicile establishment immediately

Post-move weeks 1-4:

- Execute Domicile Proof Stack checklist
- Establish local services
- Family integration begins

This countdown becomes your execution roadmap.

Coming Up

In the next chapter, we'll help you choose your specific Florida market using **The Florida Fit Matrix**. Because timing matters, but so does location. And not every Florida market works for every executive.

We'll help you match your work style, lifestyle priorities, and business needs to the right region.

But first, complete your Timing Triad exercises. Get your calendars aligned before you start house hunting. The clarity you gain will prevent expensive mistakes and create a smooth, confident transition.

As I tell every executive: timing is the difference between relocation and optimization. Both get you to Florida. Only one gets you there at the right moment.

THE FLORIDA FIT MATRIX

FINDING YOUR MARKET MATCH

EVERY EXECUTIVE KNOWS that where you operate shapes how you operate. The same job feels different in different environments. The pace, the people, the pressure. They all tune your decisions.

Relocating to Florida isn't a single choice. It's a series of micro-decisions about *fit*. The difference between thriving here and simply existing here comes down to aligning your personality, priorities, and professional rhythm with the right region.

I call that alignment **The Florida Fit Matrix**.

After my decades in Florida, watching markets rise, fall, transform, and mature - I can tell you: choosing the wrong market costs more than choosing the wrong house. You can sell a house. Changing markets means starting over.

WHEN EVERY PLACE FEELS POSSIBLE

When I first started helping peers think through their Florida moves, the conversation always began the same way. "I'm thinking Miami." Or, "Probably Tampa." Sometimes, "Somewhere quieter. Naples, maybe."

It never failed: everyone had a picture of Florida in their head, and almost none of them matched reality.

The state is more like four distinct markets than one monolithic paradise. Each has its own tempo, texture, and tribe. What fits a venture-backed founder might exhaust a CFO. What feels calm to one family might feel remote to another.

The Florida Fit Matrix helps you decode that before you buy plane tickets.

INTRODUCING THE MATRIX

The Matrix has two simple axes:

1. Business Intensity: how fast the professional and investment ecosystems move.

2. Lifestyle Balance: how much the region supports rest, community, and quality of life.

Plot those two together, and you get four natural quadrants:

Quadrant	Description	Example Cities
High Intensity / High Lifestyle	Fast-paced, network-dense markets where capital and culture collide	Miami, Brickell, Wynwood
High Intensity / Moderate Lifestyle	Ambitious metros with professional depth and livable rhythm	Tampa Bay, St. Petersburg
Moderate Intensity / High Lifestyle	Lifestyle-first regions where work follows life, not the reverse	Sarasota, Naples
Moderate Intensity / Moderate Lifestyle	Emerging metros with family affordability and steady growth	Orlando, Jacksonville

The goal isn't to rate cities. It's to help you identify which *environment* amplifies your energy instead of draining it.

HIGH INTENSITY / HIGH LIFESTYLE: THE MIAMI / SOUTH FLORIDA MODE

Miami and the surrounding South Florida region (Fort Lauderdale, Boca Raton, West Palm Beach) operate at a different frequency than the rest of Florida. This is cosmopolitan, fast-paced, and globally connected territory.

If you're raising capital, building a venture-backed company, or need regular access to international markets, South Florida's network density is unmatched in the state. The region attracts serious operators, established wealth, and international business in ways unique to Florida.

What Works Here:

- Venture capital concentration
- Latin American business connections
- Cultural amenities (arts, dining, entertainment)
- International airport infrastructure (MIA, FLL, PBI)
- Year-round energy and visibility

The Trade-offs:

- Higher cost of living and real estate prices
- Traffic and density challenges
- Constant social calendar demands
- Hurricane exposure (particularly coastal areas)
- Competitive rather than collaborative culture in some circles

Miami demands energy. The social calendar is packed, visibility matters, and the city never really slows down. Some executives thrive in that environment. Others find it exhausting after a while.

HIGH INTENSITY / MODERATE LIFESTYLE: THE TAMPA BAY / CENTRAL WEST COAST BALANCE

Tampa Bay, which includes Hillsborough County (Tampa), Pinellas County (St. Petersburg, Clearwater), and surrounding areas, has developed serious business infrastructure while maintaining livability.

The region has grown into a legitimate business hub without losing the qualities that make Florida attractive in the first place: access to water, manageable traffic, and a pace that allows you to think.

WHAT MAKES THIS MARKET WORK FOR OPERATORS:

Geographic Diversity: You can access urban centers, suburbs, and beaches within 30 minutes. That flexibility matters when balancing work calls with family life.

Airport Access: Tampa International Airport (TPA) and St. Pete-Clearwater International (PIE) provide strong connectivity. TPA in particular offers direct flights to major tech hubs and international destinations.

Relative Value: Compared to Miami or coastal California markets, Tampa Bay real estate offers better value relative to quality of life and business infrastructure.

Business Culture: The region has developed a more collaborative than cutthroat professional environment. Founders often help each other, and there's less of the status-driven competition you find in some markets.

Infrastructure Development: The region has matured significantly over recent decades with established co-working spaces, innovation hubs, university partnerships (USF, UT), and growing venture capital presence.

Year-Round Outdoor Access: Consistent climate allows for outdoor activities throughout the year. A meaningful quality-of-life factor for executives coming from harsh-winter climates.

Family-Friendly Options: The market offers both urban living (downtown Tampa, downtown St. Pete) and family-oriented neighborhoods with strong schools across both counties.

Tampa Bay at a Glance:

The region offers diverse living options across its two main counties, from historic walkable neighborhoods to waterfront communities to family-oriented suburbs. Price ranges typically run from $400K for suburban family homes to $3M+ for premium waterfront properties, with most executive-quality housing in the $600K-$1.5M range.

MODERATE INTENSITY / HIGH LIFESTYLE: THE SOUTHWEST FLORIDA MARKETS

Sarasota, Naples, Fort Myers, and the surrounding Southwest Florida region attract executives prioritizing lifestyle over business intensity. These markets have evolved beyond retirement destinations into sophisticated communities that support remote work and consulting practices.

What Works Here:

- World-class beaches and natural amenities
- Cultural institutions (Asolo Theatre, Naples Philharmonic, art galleries)
- Upscale dining and shopping
- Golf and boating communities
- Lower stress environment
- Strong healthcare infrastructure

The Trade-offs:

- Less business network density
- Fewer direct flights from smaller airports (though SRQ and RSW have improved)
- Higher proportion of seasonal residents
- Limited tech ecosystem

- Slower professional momentum

These regions work well for executives in late-career phase, consultants, board members, or those who've already built their network and can operate remotely.

You can work intensely all morning and watch the sunset in silence by five. The environment rewards focus and reflection over constant networking.

MODERATE INTENSITY / MODERATE LIFESTYLE: THE EMERGING METRO MARKETS

Orlando and Jacksonville are Florida's quiet surprises. Substantial cities with diversified economies that don't rely primarily on tourism or retirees.

Orlando Market:

- Population: 2.6M+ metro
- Strengths: Healthcare, simulation/gaming, aerospace, hospitality
- Lake Nona: Emerging life sciences and medical hub
- UCF: Large university creating talent pipeline
- Cost of living: More affordable than coastal markets
- Airport: MCO with strong connectivity
- Trade-offs: No beach access, summer heat, theme park traffic

Jacksonville Market:

- Population: 1.6M+ metro
- Strengths: Financial services, logistics, healthcare, military
- Most affordable major Florida market
- Strong business infrastructure
- Multiple beach communities (Ponte Vedra, Jacksonville Beach)
- Airport: JAX with decent connectivity

- Trade-offs: Less tech ecosystem, more corporate/traditional business culture

What These Markets Offer:

- Affordable housing relative to coastal Florida
- Strong school systems
- Established employers and stable job markets
- Lower hurricane risk (particularly Orlando)
- Room for growth and investment appreciation

These regions don't sell excitement or glamour. They sell stability, value, and long-term fundamentals. For executives prioritizing family needs, cost efficiency, and predictable growth, they deliver.

OTHER FLORIDA MARKETS WORTH EXPLORING

Beyond the major metros, Florida offers several other markets worth considering:

The Space Coast (Brevard County): Growing aerospace and tech presence around Kennedy Space Center, with beach access and lower costs than South Florida.

The Panhandle (Pensacola, Destin/30A): Emerald Coast beaches (often considered Florida's most beautiful), lower costs, growing remote worker population.

The Treasure Coast (Port St. Lucie, Vero Beach): Quieter alternative between Palm Beach and Space Coast, with golf and beach communities at lower prices.

Central Florida Polk County (Lakeland): Between Tampa and Orlando, significantly more affordable, growing logistics hub with access to both major metros.

Finding Your Fit

Choosing your market isn't about climate or coastlines. It's about matching energy.

Ask yourself:

- Do I thrive on external momentum or internal focus?
- Do I draw energy from people or from place?
- Do I want to be surrounded by ambition or insulated from it?

Each Florida market answers those questions differently.

Executives who skip this step often relocate twice; once to the wrong fit and again to the right one. You can avoid that by treating this decision as part of your strategic plan, not a real-estate hunt.

THE STORY OF TOM AND ELENA

Tom and Elena were a dual-career couple from Seattle. Tom a CTO, Elena a marketing executive. They wanted sunshine and space, but they also needed proximity to airports and strong schools.

Their first instinct was Miami. After two exploratory trips, they realized the energy felt too constant for what they wanted at this stage. They explored several other markets and eventually settled on the Tampa Bay area, specifically St. Petersburg. The community felt collaborative, the business ecosystem was growing without being overwhelming, and they could attend professional events without feeling like they were constantly networking.

Two years later, Tom still runs product for a national firm, Elena consults for startups, and their weekends are spent on the water. They call it "the right kind of busy."

Their story illustrates a key principle: there's no universally "best" Florida market. There's only the market that matches your specific priorities, pace, and life stage.

HOW TO EXPLORE WITH INTENTION

The worst way to pick a market is to rely on someone else's enthusiasm. The best way is to sample deliberately.

Plan a four-day reconnaissance trip for each potential region. Treat it like due diligence, not vacation.

Day 1: Tour neighborhoods and schools. Notice commute patterns and grocery stores, not just beaches.

Day 2: Visit co-working spaces or meet a few local professionals. See how the business energy feels.

Day 3: Test lifestyle rhythm. Exercise, walk downtown, explore dining and community events.

Day 4: Do nothing. Observe how the place feels when you stop moving.

By the end of those trips, patterns appear. Somewhere will start feeling like home.

THE SUBTLE ECONOMICS OF FIT

Every Florida market offers different trade-offs:

- **Miami/South Florida** trades higher costs and intensity for maximum network access and international connectivity
- **Tampa Bay** trades some flash and status for balanced infrastructure and relative affordability
- **Southwest Florida** trades business momentum for exceptional lifestyle and serenity
- **Orlando/Jacksonville** trade coastal location for affordability and diversified economies
- **Emerging markets** trade established ecosystems for value and growth potential

There's no wrong choice, only mismatched expectations.

Executives who treat market selection as a strategic variable, not an afterthought, make cleaner, happier moves. They stop comparing based on other people's priorities and start designing their own ecosystem.

Your job is to identify where your energy multiplies instead of drains. That's your Florida Fit.

ACTION PLAN: FINDING YOUR FIT

1. Plot Yourself on the Florida Fit Matrix (15 minutes)

Rate your own *Business Intensity* preference (1-10, where 10 = constant action and networking) and *Lifestyle Balance* preference (1-10, where 10 = maximum relaxation and family time).

Plot yourself on the matrix. Which quadrant do you fall into naturally?

Success metric: You can clearly articulate whether you need high-energy business environment or prefer slower pace.

2. Shortlist Two Markets Based on Your Matrix Position (30 minutes)

Based on your self-assessment, identify two Florida markets that align with your scores.

For each market, write down:

- What attracts you about this market's energy level?
- What concerns you about potential downsides?
- Which aspect matters most: business network, lifestyle quality, or cost?

Success metric: You have two specific markets to research, not vague "somewhere in Florida."

3. Schedule Reconnaissance Trips with Clear Goals (2 hours planning)

Book 4-day trips to your two shortlisted markets. Don't combine them, each market deserves focused attention.

For each trip, schedule:

- Day 1: Neighborhood tours (plan 3-4 different areas to visit)
- Day 2: Business immersion (co-working space visit, coffee with a local executive if possible)
- Day 3: Lifestyle testing (work out, walk around, eat locally, observe daily rhythms)
- Day 4: Do nothing (see how the place feels when you're not in tourism mode)

Success metric: Two trips booked with specific daily intentions, not generic "house hunting."

4. Create Your Must-Have Criteria List (30 minutes)

List your five non-negotiable factors. Common examples:

- Airport direct flights to [specific cities]
- Top 10% schools for [grade levels]
- Beach access within [X minutes]
- Active tech/business community
- Cost of living under $[X] per month

Rank them 1-5 in order of importance.

Success metric: You can objectively score each market against your criteria rather than making emotional decisions.

5. Interview Three Local Residents in Each Market (2-3 weeks)

Find executives already living in your shortlisted markets. Ask them:

- What surprised you most after moving?
- What do you wish you'd known before relocating?
- How long did it take to feel integrated?
- What's the hidden cost or challenge nobody mentions?
- Would you make the same choice again?

Success metric: You've heard firsthand accounts from people who've already made the move, not just real estate marketing.

6. Decide Your Primary Trade-Off (30 minutes reflection)

Every Florida market asks you to trade something. Identify what you're most willing to sacrifice:

- Speed and network density (for calmer pace)
- Waterfront lifestyle (for better schools or lower cost)
- Urban walkability (for space and newer construction)
- Established community (for emerging market with growth potential)

Write down: "I'm willing to trade [X] for [Y] because [reason]."

Success metric: You've made a conscious trade-off decision rather than hoping you can have everything.

7. Assess the Insider Advantage (15 minutes)

Ask yourself: Would working with someone who has spent decades in this market, someone who knows where executives actually succeed, which neighborhoods have staying power, and how to time the market strategically, improve my outcome?

If yes, reach out to advisors who understand both your world and Florida's reality.

If no, at minimum connect with local executives before making any commitments.

Success metric: You've acknowledged whether local expertise would de-risk your move and improve your results.

8. Build Your Final Decision Matrix (1 hour)

Create a simple spreadsheet:

- Rows: Your shortlisted markets
- Columns: Your must-have criteria (from Exercise 4)

- Scores: Rate each market 1-10 on each criterion
- Weight: Multiply by importance ranking
- Total: Sum weighted scores

The math doesn't make the decision for you, but it clarifies which market objectively fits your priorities.

Success metric: You have a documented, rational basis for your market selection that you can explain to family, advisors, and yourself.

Coming Up Next

In the next chapter, we'll shift from *where* to *how*. Specifically, how to build your network flywheel before you've even unpacked. Because Florida's most successful relocations aren't about finding the right house. They're about finding your people and integrating strategically from day one.

But first, complete your Florida Fit Matrix exercises. Understanding which market matches your operating style prevents expensive mistakes and creates a foundation for everything else.

As I tell every executive: location is more than geography. It's the environment that either amplifies or drains your energy. Choose accordingly.

BUILD YOUR
NETWORK FLYWHEEL

FROM STRANGER TO INSIDER IN 90 DAYS

THE BOXES AREN'T EVEN OPEN YET, and you're already thinking about who you know here. That's good instinct. Most executives underestimate how long it takes to rebuild social capital.

You may have moved for lifestyle, but your network determines how fast you integrate. A move without relationships is just geography. A move with a network becomes opportunity.

The fastest way to turn a new city into a real home is to build what I call **The Network Flywheel**. A system that keeps relationships moving, compounding, and returning value long after the introductions fade.

Over the years in Tampa Bay, I've watched hundreds of executives navigate this transition. The ones who integrate fastest treat networking like a product launch: systematic, intentional, and measured. The ones who struggle treat it as something that will "happen naturally" once they settle in.

It doesn't. You have to build it.

THE SIX-MONTH SILENCE

When most executives relocate, they go quiet.

They spend the first six months settling in, organizing, catching up on work. They tell themselves they'll network "once things calm down." But things never calm down.

Then one day, they look up and realize they've built a great house but no professional life around it. The phone doesn't ring because no one knows they're there.

The problem isn't Florida. It's inertia.

A move resets your credibility clock. The people who knew your track record are hundreds of miles away. The people here only know what you show them.

That's why networking after relocation isn't about starting over. It's about restarting momentum, and you do that by giving before asking.

THE NETWORK FLYWHEEL

A flywheel stores energy and releases it through consistent motion. Your network works the same way.

Each small act of contribution adds force. Over time, the motion sustains itself.

Here's the framework:

1. Give Value First

2. Join with Purpose

3. Connect Consistently

4. Be Visible

5. Be Invited Back

Follow these steps, and relationships start working for you instead of you working for them.

GIVE VALUE FIRST

The best connectors in any market share a common habit: they help early.

When you meet someone, think about how you can add something useful right away; an introduction, a resource, an idea, or even just genuine curiosity.

Florida's professional culture values generosity. People here notice who contributes without agenda. The fastest way to get included is to be the one who helps others integrate.

That doesn't mean overextending. It means leading with initiative. The difference between a stranger and a contact is often one helpful email.

In my experience working with executives across Tampa Bay, the ones who succeed fastest are the ones who show up asking "how can I help?" before they ask "can you help me?"

JOIN WITH PURPOSE

Every executive needs three kinds of communities:

1. Professional: Industry or functional groups where you stay sharp.

2. Civic: Local organizations where you invest in the region's growth.

3. Social: Groups or hobbies that connect you to people beyond work.

Each serves a different role. Professional keeps you credible. Civic keeps you connected. Social keeps you sane.

When you relocate, pick one of each intentionally. Too many newcomers join everything, hoping to accelerate belonging. That leads to burnout and shallow ties.

The goal isn't volume; it's velocity. A few right circles create exponential reach.

CONNECT CONSISTENTLY

Networking isn't an event. It's a rhythm.

Schedule time for relationship maintenance just like you would for a leadership meeting. Even two short coffees a week add up to a strong foundation in six months.

The key is consistency. When people see you show up regularly, they start associating you with reliability. Consistency compounds faster than charisma.

If you're naturally introverted, consistency helps even more. You don't have to be everywhere; you just have to be present enough to be remembered.

BE VISIBLE

Florida is full of talented people who stay invisible. They assume that because they're experienced, word will spread. But in a new market, reputation doesn't precede you. It follows effort.

Visibility isn't self-promotion. It's participation.

Speak on a panel. Write a short piece on LinkedIn about what you're learning in your transition. Volunteer as a mentor at a local incubator or university. Attend a chamber event not to pitch, but to listen and contribute insight.

Visibility creates serendipity. It lets people find you who didn't know to look.

BE INVITED BACK

You'll know your network flywheel is working when people start reaching out first.

The second invitation is always the proof of value.

When peers include you in projects, events, or conversations without you asking, it means your reputation has converted from novelty to trust.

At that point, networking stops being effort and starts being ecosystem. You're no longer the new person. You're part of the fabric.

That's the moment relocation turns into belonging.

THE STORY OF JEFF

Jeff was a Chief Information Security Officer who relocated from Chicago to Tampa Bay. Smart, experienced, deeply networked back home, but cautious about starting over.

For the first few months, he kept his head down. He figured his Chicago contacts would sustain him while he got settled. They didn't. When his company started expanding regionally, he realized he didn't know anyone local to recommend or partner with.

So he decided to reverse the approach. He started hosting small breakfasts every Friday at a local café in Hyde Park. No agenda, just peers swapping ideas. The first one had three people. A year later, there were twenty regulars, including local investors and startup founders.

Jeff's role didn't change, but his reach did. He didn't network harder. He networked with intention.

THE FLORIDA FACTOR

Florida's business culture is deceptively open. People will meet you for coffee faster than in most cities. But they'll only remember you if you follow through.

Many executives find the state refreshingly accessible. You can get to interesting people quickly. The challenge is depth. Because so many newcomers arrive every month, the relationships that endure are the ones built on real contribution.

Show up consistently. Add value early. Keep your word. In this market, reliability stands out more than titles. I've watched the same pattern: executives who treat Florida like a transaction struggle. Executives who treat it like a community thrive.

DIGITAL MEETS LOCAL

The hybrid nature of modern networking works in your favor. You can blend digital presence with real-world engagement.

Use LinkedIn as your professional storefront. Post insights, highlight local wins, and comment thoughtfully on others' work. Then back it up with actual attendance at events and direct follow-ups.

Digital presence attracts awareness. Local engagement builds trust.

The combination makes you visible to both old contacts and new ones, creating bridges that make relocation exponential instead of linear.

THE MINDSET SHIFT

The executives who build thriving networks here don't see it as self-promotion. They see it as stewardship.

Every introduction you make or event you support adds momentum to the ecosystem. That's what Florida rewards: people who help the community grow instead of waiting for it to serve them.

Once that mindset clicks, networking stops being a chore. It becomes a competitive advantage.

I've watched this transformation happen dozens of times. Executives arrive thinking "I need to network to build my business." Six months later, they're thinking "I network because I enjoy contributing to this community." That's when the Flywheel really accelerates.

THE FEEDBACK LOOP

The Network Flywheel creates a loop of visibility and credibility. The more you participate, the more people associate your name with contribution. That awareness leads to invitations, which lead to more opportunities to give value.

At that point, the system sustains itself. You don't chase connections. They compound naturally.

One executive told me: "In New York, I spent 40% of my energy just maintaining my network. Here, the network maintains itself because everyone's genuinely helpful."

That's the Tampa Bay advantage. But you have to earn it by showing up and contributing first.

ACTION PLAN: BUILD YOUR NETWORK FLYWHEEL

Work through these exercises to build systematic network momentum:

1. Identify Your Three Communities (1 hour)

Decide which one professional, one civic, and one social community you'll join within your first 60 days.

Professional: (industry / functional group)

- Options: Tampa Bay Tech Forum, CFO Alliance, industry-specific associations
- Criteria: meets monthly, has active membership, attracts people at your level
- Your choice: _____

Civic: (local impact organization)

- Options: United Way, educational institution involvement, economic development council

- Criteria: aligns with your values, has board/volunteer opportunities, respected locally
- Your choice: _____

Social: (hobby or lifestyle group)

- Options: running club, sailing group, co-working community, arts patron group
- Criteria: genuinely interests you, meets regularly, builds real friendships
- Your choice: _____

Success metric: You've committed to three specific groups within 60 days of arrival.

2. Create Your Weekly Networking Cadence (30 minutes)

Schedule recurring time for relationship building, just like you would for team meetings.

Weekly commitment:

- Two 30-minute coffee meetings (1 hour total)
- One networking event or group meeting (2 hours)
- 30 minutes of LinkedIn engagement (commenting, posting, connecting)
- 30 minutes of follow-up emails and relationship maintenance

Total weekly investment: 4 hours

Block this time on your calendar now, recurring for the next 6 months.

Success metric: Networking becomes routine, not something you "fit in when there's time."

3. Build Your Value-Add List (30 minutes)

Create a simple list of ways you can help others. Update it monthly as you learn more about the local ecosystem.

Categories:

- Introductions I can make (to people in your network, even if not local yet)
- Expertise I can share (speak at events, mentor, advise)
- Resources I can provide (templates, tools, insights from your career)
- Platforms I can offer (podcast guest spots, guest posts, panel participation)

Keep this list handy. Reference it when you meet new people. Leading with value creates reciprocity naturally.

4. Schedule Your First Event Attendance (immediate)

Within the next 7 days, attend one local business event.

Where to find events:

- Tampa Bay Business Journal events calendar
- Eventbrite search: "Tampa Bay professional" or "St Petersburg business"
- LinkedIn events in your area
- Chamber of commerce calendars
- Industry association events

Event protocol:

- Set a goal of 3 meaningful conversations (not 20 business cards)
- Ask questions, don't pitch
- Follow up within 48 hours with anyone interesting
- Post a brief LinkedIn update about what you learned

Success metric: You attend your first event within one week of deciding to relocate.

5. Commit to One "Give First" Action Weekly (ongoing)

Every week, do one thing that helps someone else with zero expectation of return.

Examples:

- Make an introduction between two people who should know each other
- Share a relevant article or resource with someone
- Offer feedback on someone's project or pitch
- Connect someone to a resource they need
- Write a LinkedIn recommendation for someone
- Invite someone to an event they'd find valuable

Track these actions. They compound faster than you expect.

6. Leverage Available Networks (when ready)

If you're working with a real estate advisor or other professionals on your relocation, ask about network introductions:

- Initial conversation: Share your professional background, interests, and what you're building in Florida
- Request targeted introductions to 3-5 key people in your industry or function area
- Based on how those initial conversations go, ask for strategic second-tier introductions
- Within 90 days: You should be plugged into relevant networks and operating independently

Your commitment: Show up, follow through, and pay it forward by helping the next person who relocates.

Coming Up

In the next chapter, we'll discuss **Real Estate as a Strategy**: how to think about property not as a purchase but as a portfolio. We'll cover the Anchor/Growth/Freedom framework and show you how to build wealth while building your Florida life.

But first, execute your Network Flywheel plan. Because relationships determine how fast everything else falls into place.

As I tell every executive: your network isn't what you know. It's who trusts you. Build trust through contribution, and everything else follows.

REAL ESTATE AS A STRATEGY (BUILDING YOUR PROPERTY PORTFOLIO)

IF YOU WANT to understand the difference between moving to Florida and building a life here, it comes down to one thing: real estate.

For most people, buying a house is about lifestyle. For executives, it's about structure. Where you live becomes the foundation for how you live. It anchors your identity, stabilizes your domicile, and influences every financial decision that follows.

Too many smart people treat real estate like a single event. They pick a home, close a deal, and move on. But real estate isn't a transaction. It's a system. One that can work for or against you depending on how deliberately you design it.

You wouldn't launch a product without understanding how it fits your portfolio. The same rule applies here. Your property decisions should work together, not in isolation.

I call this approach **The Property Portfolio Layers**: Anchor, Growth, and Freedom.

THE STORY OF THE EARLY BUYER

When Steve moved from New York to Miami, he did everything right on paper. He sold his Manhattan apartment, timed the move around bonuses, and established domicile properly.

What he didn't plan for was the emotional rush that hit once he arrived. Within three weeks, he bought a waterfront condo in Brickell that looked perfect in photos. By month six, he realized it wasn't the right fit for his daily life; noise from the street, limited parking, and a social scene that exhausted rather than energized him.

He'd optimized for image, not function.

It wasn't a mistake so much as a missed opportunity. Had he slowed down and treated the purchase as part of a broader plan, he could have aligned his real estate with his actual goals instead of his immediate excitement.

The right real estate strategy protects you from that impulse.

THE PROPERTY PORTFOLIO LAYERS

This framework turns real estate into an integrated system rather than a single decision. Each layer serves a purpose.

1. **Anchor**: your base of operations
2. **Growth**: your engine for wealth and diversification
3. **Freedom**: your expression of lifestyle and legacy

Let's unpack them.

Anchor: The Foundation

Your **Anchor** property is your home base. The center of your Florida life. It's where you register to vote, pay taxes, receive mail, and build community.

The Anchor is both emotional and functional. It grounds your relocation and validates your domicile. It's where you live, think, and recharge.

Choosing your Anchor well means balancing identity and practicality.

Ask yourself:

- Does this home align with how I actually live, not just how I imagine living?
- Is it close to the people, schools, and airports that matter?
- Can I sustain it comfortably through market cycles?
- Does it support my work requirements (home office, quiet, connectivity)?

The best Anchors are not necessarily the most glamorous. They are the most *enduring*.

A good Anchor gives you permanence without rigidity. It should make you feel planted but not trapped.

When your Anchor is solid, everything else. Your network, finances, and rhythm begins to compound.

ANCHOR PROPERTY CONSIDERATIONS ACROSS FLORIDA MARKETS

Different Florida markets offer different Anchor advantages:

South Florida (Miami, Fort Lauderdale, Boca Raton, West Palm Beach)

- **Best for**: Executives needing international connectivity, frequent travel
- **Anchor advantages**: Direct flights worldwide, cultural amenities, established wealth management ecosystem
- **Anchor challenges**: Highest costs, traffic density, hurricane exposure
- **Typical Anchor investment**: $800K–$3M+ depending on location and lifestyle needs

Tampa Bay (Tampa, St. Petersburg, Clearwater)

- **Best for**: Executives balancing business intensity with lifestyle quality
- **Anchor advantages**: TPA airport access, geographic diversity (urban/suburban/beach within 30 minutes), still-reasonable costs
- **Anchor challenges**: Growing rapidly (pricing rising), insurance costs increasing
- **Typical Anchor investment**: $500K–$2M+ depending on neighborhood and water access

Southwest Florida (Sarasota, Naples, Fort Myers)

- **Best for**: Executives prioritizing lifestyle, later career stage, consultants
- **Anchor advantages**: World-class beaches, cultural amenities, lower stress
- **Anchor challenges**: Fewer direct flights, seasonal population swings, less business density
- **Typical Anchor investment**: $600K–$2.5M+ depending on market and water proximity

Orlando Metro

- **Best for**: Families prioritizing schools and affordability, executives with flexible travel
- **Anchor advantages**: Most affordable major Florida market, strong job market, excellent schools
- **Anchor challenges**: No beach access, summer heat intensity, theme park traffic
- **Typical Anchor investment**: $400K–$800K for executive-quality housing

Jacksonville

- **Best for**: Value-oriented executives, those prioritizing space and traditional business culture
- **Anchor advantages**: Most affordable coastal Florida option, beach communities available, strong military/corporate presence
- **Anchor challenges**: Less tech ecosystem, more traditional business culture
- **Typical Anchor investment**: $350K–$700K for quality executive housing

GROWTH: THE ENGINE

Once your Anchor is secure, you can think about the **Growth** layer. The properties that generate income, build equity, or serve as strategic assets.

For some, this means buying a rental property in a high-demand area. For others, it's a short-term vacation rental that doubles as a personal retreat. For a few, it's a calculated investment in emerging neighborhoods or development zones.

The Growth layer isn't about speculation. It's about steady, compounding leverage.

Florida's sustained migration has created consistent housing demand across the state. That demand translates into opportunity, but only for those who manage it professionally.

Treat investment properties like business units. Analyze cash flow, maintenance costs, property management, tenant demand, and risk the way you would any profit center.

A managed rental portfolio, handled correctly, can offset carrying costs of your Anchor and create future passive income. It also keeps you connected to Florida's economic pulse. You start to understand the market not as a consumer but as an investor.

GROWTH PROPERTY STRATEGIES BY MARKET

Miami / South Florida Growth Opportunities:

- **Strategy**: Urban condos for long-term rentals to young professionals, international buyers
- **Advantages**: Highest rent yields in Florida, strong international demand
- **Challenges**: Highest purchase prices, HOA complexity, seasonal vacancy risk
- **Typical approach**: Purchase $400K–$700K condo, rent for $2,800–$4,500/month

Tampa Bay Growth Opportunities:

- **Strategy**: Rental homes near USF/UT, condos in downtown St. Pete, emerging neighborhood plays
- **Advantages**: Strong rental demand, diverse tenant base (students, young professionals, relocating executives)
- **Challenges**: Insurance costs rising, market heating up
- **Typical approach**: Purchase $350K–$600K property, rent for $2,200–$3,500/month

Orlando Growth Opportunities:

- **Strategy**: Vacation rental properties near theme parks, long-term rentals near UCF or Lake Nona
- **Advantages**: Dual-use potential (vacation rental + personal use), strong tourism demand
- **Challenges**: Short-term rental regulations changing, seasonal income variability
- **Typical approach**: Purchase $300K–$500K property, generate $40K–$70K annual rental income

Southwest Florida Growth Opportunities:

- **Strategy**: Seasonal rentals (snowbird market), luxury vacation rentals
- **Advantages**: Premium rental rates during season, personal use in off-season
- **Challenges**: Vacancy in summer months, high-end market volatility
- **Typical approach**: Purchase $500K–$1M property, target $60K–$100K seasonal rental income

Jacksonville / Emerging Markets Growth Opportunities:

- **Strategy**: Value plays in appreciating neighborhoods, multi-family properties
- **Advantages**: Lower entry costs, strong military / corporate tenant base, better cash flow
- **Challenges**: Slower appreciation, limited tourist rental demand
- **Typical approach**: Purchase $250K–$400K property, rent for $1,800–$2,800/month

FREEDOM: THE ASPIRATIONAL LAYER

The **Freedom** property is the one that reminds you why you made the move in the first place.

It might be a coastal retreat, a lake cabin, or a space that supports a hobby or family tradition. Sometimes it's not a property you own yet. It's the one you're building toward.

Freedom properties are emotional investments. They signal a shift from survival to satisfaction.

They're also your future flexibility. Many executives use Freedom properties as early legacy plays. A place where family gathers or where they test semi-retirement patterns.

When planned wisely, Freedom assets become the emotional dividend of a well-executed relocation.

FREEDOM PROPERTY EXAMPLES ACROSS FLORIDA

Coastal Freedom Properties:

- Gulf Coast beaches (Clearwater, St. Pete Beach, Anna Maria Island, Sanibel, 30A)
- Atlantic beaches (Ponte Vedra, Vero Beach, Melbourne Beach)
- Typical investment: $600K–$2M+ for beachfront/near-beach cottage or condo

Lake and Nature Freedom Properties:

- Central Florida lakes (Clermont, Mount Dora)
- Inland waterfront (various locations statewide)
- Rural retreats (horse properties, acreage in North Florida)
- Typical investment: $300K–$800K for recreational property

Urban Freedom Properties:

- Downtown loft/condo for weekends in the city (if your Anchor is suburban)
- Walkable neighborhood home in arts districts
- Typical investment: $300K–$700K for urban retreat

INTEGRATING THE LAYERS

These three layers aren't sequential steps; they're interlocking parts of one system.

Your Anchor grounds your identity.

Your Growth layer funds your future.

Your Freedom layer fuels your motivation.

When all three work together, your life and portfolio reinforce each other.

It doesn't matter whether your Anchor is a downtown Tampa condo or a family home in Jacksonville's Ponte Vedra, or whether your Growth play is a duplex in Orlando or a beach rental in Naples. What matters is intent.

The moment you design your real estate around purpose instead of impulse, you've turned relocation into a long-term strategy.

REAL EXECUTIVE EXAMPLES ACROSS FLORIDA

Julia: The Sarasota Three-Layer Portfolio

Julia was a product executive from Boston who moved to Sarasota. Her strategy evolved systematically:

Year 1 - Anchor: Modest single-family home in walkable Sarasota neighborhood. $650K investment.

Year 2 - Growth: Rental townhouse near colleges. $380K investment, $2,400/month rent.

Year 3-4 - Freedom: Small Siesta Key cottage for weekends and seasonal rental. $850K investment, $40K/year income when not using personally.

Total portfolio: $1.88M. The Growth and Freedom properties cover her Anchor costs.

Marcus: The Miami Urban + Airbnb Strategy

Marcus was CTO of a cybersecurity company who relocated from San Francisco to Miami. His approach was more aggressive:

Anchor: Downtown Brickell condo, $1.2M. Walking distance to restaurants, offices, waterfront.

Growth 1: Edgewater condo for Airbnb. $550K investment, generates $65K/year.

Growth 2: West Palm Beach single-family rental. $480K investment, $3,200/month.

Total portfolio: $2.23M

Annual rental income: ~$103K

David: The Jacksonville Value Play

David was CFO of a logistics company who moved from Chicago to Jacksonville:

Anchor: Ponte Vedra Beach home, $625K. Beach access, golf, excellent schools.

Growth 1: Arlington rental, $285K. $2,100/month to military family.

Growth 2: Riverside duplex, $340K. Two units at $1,450/month each.

Growth 3: Small retail property, $420K. $3,500/month commercial lease.

Total portfolio: $1.67M

Annual rental income: ~$84K

The Florida Insurance Reality

One of the biggest adjustments for new Florida residents is understanding the insurance landscape.

Florida's weather patterns, particularly hurricanes, create an insurance market that works differently than most states. Premiums vary dramatically based on multiple factors, and the market has become more volatile in recent years.

UNDERSTANDING FLORIDA INSURANCE COSTS

Coastal vs. Inland Reality:

Coastal properties (within a few miles of saltwater):

- Wind/hurricane coverage: $8,000–$25,000+ annually for typical executive home
- Flood insurance (if in flood zone): $1,500–$6,000+ annually
- Total insurance carry: $10,000–$30,000+ annually common

Near-coastal properties (5-15 miles inland):

- Wind/hurricane coverage: $4,000–$12,000 annually
- Flood insurance (varies greatly by elevation): $800–$3,000 annually
- Total insurance carry: $5,000–$15,000 annually typical

Inland properties (Central Florida, Jacksonville inland):

- Standard homeowner's: $2,500–$6,000 annually
- Flood insurance (usually not required): $500–$1,500 if needed
- Total insurance carry: $3,000–$7,500 annually typical

FACTORS THAT IMPACT YOUR PREMIUMS

1. **Roof age and type**: New roof with impact-resistant shingles = significant discount
2. **Wind mitigation features**: Hurricane shutters, impact windows, reinforced doors
3. **Distance from coast**: Even 5 miles makes a major difference
4. **Flood zone**: Zone X (minimal risk) vs. Zone A/V (high risk) = 3-5x cost difference
5. **Construction type**: CBS (concrete block/stucco) vs. frame construction
6. **Claims history**: Both personal and property history matters

INSURANCE STRATEGY FOR YOUR PORTFOLIO

For Your Anchor:

- Get quotes from multiple carriers before purchasing

- Consider wind mitigation improvements as investment, not expense
- Understand whether you're in a flood zone (this affects financing too)
- Budget realistically. Insurance is often your second-highest monthly cost after mortgage

For Growth Properties:

- Factor insurance into cash flow analysis (it's often underestimated)
- Vacant property insurance is more expensive. Factor this for vacation rentals
- Landlord policies have different requirements than homeowner's
- Consider umbrella liability coverage across your portfolio

Red Flags to Investigate:

- Home hasn't had roof replaced in 15+ years (replacement often required for insurance)
- Property in flood Zone A or V without adequate elevation
- Previous major claims on the property
- Citizens Property Insurance (state-run insurer of last resort) signals insurability issues

WORKING WITH INSURANCE PROFESSIONALS

Before making any Florida property purchase:

1. **Get a preliminary insurance quote** using the property address
2. **Request a wind mitigation inspection report** if buying (seller should provide)
3. **Order a flood elevation certificate** if property is near flood zones

4. **Work with a Florida-experienced insurance broker** who knows multiple carriers

Don't wait until closing to think about insurance. In Florida, insurance can make or break a deal, or significantly impact your ROI calculations.

THE REAL ESTATE TEAM

Your real estate portfolio requires a coordinated team, not just a single agent.

At minimum, you'll want:

Real Estate Advisor

- Someone who understands executive relocation dynamics
- Experience with investment property analysis
- Knowledge of multiple Florida markets if you're building a portfolio
- Ability to coordinate timing around your equity events and tax strategy

Property Insurance Broker

- Florida-specific experience essential
- Access to multiple carriers (not just one company)
- Understanding of wind mitigation and flood requirements
- Ability to handle both personal and investment property needs

Property Manager (for Growth properties)

- Licensed and insured in Florida
- Experience with your property type (long-term vs. short-term)
- Financial transparency and regular reporting
- Maintenance network already established

Real Estate Attorney

- Florida bar admission
- Experience with investment properties and landlord law
- Can review complex transactions and multi-property strategies
- Coordinates with your tax advisor on entity structure

Financial Planner/CPA

- Understands real estate tax implications
- Can advise on entity structure (LLC, etc.)
- Integrates property portfolio into overall wealth strategy
- Coordinates timing of purchases with your income and tax situation

You don't need a massive team, just a coordinated one who understand they're working together.

WHY MARKET KNOWLEDGE MATTERS

Successful property portfolio strategies require working with professionals who understand both real estate investment analysis and executive relocation dynamics. After years observing Florida markets, the patterns are clear: which neighborhoods have staying power versus temporary hype, where infrastructure improvements will drive appreciation, and which properties will actually cash flow once you account for all costs. This knowledge doesn't come from MLS data, it comes from living through multiple real estate cycles.

THE LONG VIEW

Real estate reflects identity and strategy. How you choose to structure your property portfolio says as much about your approach to wealth building as your investment decisions do.

When you treat property decisions as part of a broader plan, you start to see Florida not just as a destination but as a platform. A place where your personal and financial architectures align.

You stop reacting to market conditions and start designing around them.

That's when relocation becomes true wealth creation.

ACTION PLAN: DESIGNING YOUR PROPERTY PORTFOLIO

1. Define Your Anchor Criteria (1 hour)

Before looking at properties, write down your Anchor non-negotiables:

- Commute requirements (airport, office, co-working)
- School needs (if applicable)
- Lifestyle priorities (walkable, water access, golf, etc.)
- Budget including realistic insurance costs
- Domicile considerations (primary residence requirements)

Success metric: You have clear written criteria before viewing properties.

2. Analyze Potential Growth Opportunities (2-3 hours)

If considering investment properties, create a simple analysis for each:

- Purchase price + renovation costs
- Estimated rental income (monthly or seasonal)
- Operating expenses (property management, insurance, maintenance, HOA, property taxes)
- Vacancy assumptions
- Cash flow after all expenses
- Appreciation potential based on neighborhood trends

Success metric: You can calculate whether a Growth property actually makes financial sense before buying.

3. Envision Your Freedom Property (30 minutes reflection)

Even if you're not ready to buy it yet, define what your Freedom property represents:

- Where would it be located?
- How would you use it (weekends, seasons, family gatherings)?
- What does it symbolize about your successful relocation?
- When do you realistically plan to acquire it?

Success metric: You have a clear aspiration that motivates your overall Florida strategy.

4. Get Preliminary Insurance Quotes (2-3 hours)

Before making offers on any Florida property:

- Contact 2-3 Florida insurance brokers
- Provide property addresses you're considering
- Request quotes including wind/hurricane and flood (if applicable)
- Ask about wind mitigation discounts
- Factor real costs into your purchase decision

Success metric: No insurance surprises at closing; realistic carrying cost expectations.

5. Build Your Property Team Roster (ongoing)

Create a contact list of your real estate team:

- Real estate advisor (with Florida portfolio experience)
- Insurance broker (Florida-specific)
- Property manager (if needed for rentals)
- Real estate attorney (Florida bar)
- CPA/financial advisor (understands Florida property strategy)

For each, document:

- How you found them
- What they specialize in
- Communication preferences
- Fee structures

Success metric: You have a coordinated team, not just isolated service providers.

6. Schedule Market Research Trips (if considering multi-property strategy)

If you're thinking about properties in different Florida markets:

- Plan 2-3 day visits to each target market
- Drive neighborhoods at different times of day
- Talk to property managers about local rental markets
- Visit areas where you'd actually want to own, not just tourist areas
- Meet with local real estate professionals who know investment properties

Success metric: You understand multiple Florida markets firsthand, not just from online research.

7. Create a 5-Year Property Acquisition Timeline (1 hour)

Map out your property portfolio evolution:

- Year 1: Anchor established
- Year 2-3: Consider first Growth property?
- Year 3-5: Freedom property acquisition?

Include:

- Financial milestones required for each purchase
- Life events that might affect timing

- Market conditions to monitor

Success metric: You have a multi-year vision for your Florida real estate portfolio, not just your next purchase.

8. Annual Portfolio Review Process (quarterly, 30 minutes)

Every quarter, review your property portfolio:

- Is my Anchor still aligned with my life/work?
- Are Growth properties performing as projected?
- What's my total real estate allocation vs. other investments?
- Am I ready for the next layer?
- Do I need to adjust my strategy based on market changes?

Success metric: Your real estate strategy evolves with your life and stays aligned with your goals.

Coming Up Next

In the next chapter, we'll discuss selecting the right advisors. The people who can help you execute this property strategy and your broader Florida relocation successfully. Because having the right frameworks is one thing. Having the right team to implement them is what separates good moves from great ones.

But first, complete your property portfolio planning exercises. Understanding your Anchor, Growth, and Freedom strategy prevents expensive mistakes and creates a foundation for long-term wealth building in Florida.

As I tell every executive: real estate isn't about finding the perfect property. It's about designing a property system that supports the life you're building.

SELECTING THE RIGHT ADVISOR (BUILDING YOUR RELOCATION TEAM)

EVERY RELOCATION SUCCEEDS or struggles on the quality of your team.

You can do everything right on paper; pick the right market, time it perfectly, even buy smart, but if your advisors are misaligned, the experience will still feel harder than it should.

The right people make the process lighter, faster, and smarter. The wrong ones drain energy and trust.

Executives know this instinctively inside their companies. We hire for alignment, not just ability. Yet when it comes to personal transitions, we often forget that lesson and choose whoever answers the phone first or comes recommended by someone who doesn't really understand what we need.

In Florida, relationships move everything forward. Advisors are your local operating system. Choose them like you would your leadership team.

THE STORY OF THE PERFECTLY WRONG FIT

When Emily, a Chief Marketing Officer from New Jersey, decided to relocate to Florida, she called a friend who "knew a great realtor." The agent was experienced, professional, and highly rated.

What Emily didn't realize was that this agent specialized in vacation properties and retiree relocations, not executive relocations. The advice was centered on views and lifestyle amenities, not on the complex logistics of maintaining domicile, timing around equity events, or building a professional network.

Emily needed help navigating school districts that would work for her family, understanding how her move timing would affect her stock vesting schedule, getting introductions to other executives in her industry, and coordinating with her CPA on domicile documentation.

Instead, she got a competent agent who showed her beautiful homes but couldn't advise on any of the strategic questions that actually mattered for her situation.

The result was a home she loved but a transition that felt disjointed and lonely. She figured out the important stuff eventually, but it took months longer and cost more (in both dollars and stress) than it should have.

The problem wasn't competence. It was context. The advisor understood real estate transactions, not executive relocation strategy.

Florida has thousands of skilled professionals. What matters is finding the ones who understand your world. People who can think strategically about how lifestyle, finance, timing, domicile, network, and property all interconnect.

THE ADVISOR SPECTRUM

The best way to think about your support team is as a spectrum with three distinct functions: **Agent, Advisor, and Connector.**

Each plays a role. Sometimes one person fills multiple functions. The goal is not assembling a large team; it's gaining clarity about what you need and matching people to those specific needs.

1. The Agent: Transactional Support

Agents execute. They move deals from listing to closing. They handle paperwork, negotiations, inspections, and deadlines.

Every relocation needs one. But the best agents for executives do more than open doors, They manage process with precision. They respect confidentiality, anticipate complexity, and communicate like peers rather than clients.

When evaluating an agent, ask yourself:

- Do they understand the business and financial implications of my move?
- Have they worked with people in similar roles or life stages?
- Can they coordinate across other advisors, like attorneys or accountants?
- Do they understand how equity events, bonuses, and tax timing affect purchase decisions?

A good agent manages the transaction. A great one manages the transition.

Look for professionals who listen more than they talk. Ask how they handle out-of-state buyers, remote closings, and multiple-property strategies. Their answers will tell you whether they think like an operator or like a salesperson.

Red flags with agents:

- Pushing you toward properties based on their commission structure
- Unable to explain market trends or neighborhood evolution
- No experience coordinating with CPAs or attorneys on timing

- Dismissive of your concerns about domicile, schools, or network
- Focused only on this transaction, not your long-term Florida strategy

2. The Advisor: Strategic Alignment

Advisors go beyond execution. They see the bigger picture and understand how each decision creates ripple effects.

A relocation-savvy advisor understands that every choice has secondary implications: tax consequences, timing considerations, insurance complexity, domicile proof, and estate planning integration. They help you make decisions that serve your broader goals, not just your immediate wants.

In real estate, that might mean steering you toward a neighborhood with stronger long-term fundamentals, even if it's less flashy today. It could mean advising you to wait three months to establish domicile before purchasing, even though you're ready to buy now. It might involve helping you think about whether your first property should be your Anchor or if you should rent initially while you explore different areas.

In financial planning, it involves structuring ownership under the right entity, coordinating purchase timing with your income recognition, and thinking about how this property fits into your overall wealth strategy.

In legal terms, it means ensuring your domicile proof stays consistent across all documentation and that your estate planning reflects your new Florida residency.

Advisors protect you from short-term thinking.

You'll know you've found a true advisor when they ask questions that surprise you. Not about square footage and amenities, but about your life design. Where do you travel most frequently? How do you actually work day to day? What does freedom look like for you five years from now? What's your exit strategy if this doesn't work out?

Those aren't small talk questions. They're strategy questions that reveal whether someone is thinking transactionally or holistically.

3. The Connector: Ecosystem Integration

The Connector is the rare person who doesn't just help you land; they help you launch.

Connectors introduce you to the ecosystem: other executives, investors, community leaders, and local professionals who operate at your level. They know where value lives in the relationships around you, not just in the transactions.

In Florida, this layer matters more than most people realize. The business community here is highly networked but geographically distributed. You can't just walk into "the tech hub" or "the finance district" because they're spread across different cities and even different coasts.

The right introduction can accelerate your sense of belonging and your professional integration by months. The wrong approach, trying to network broadly without warm introductions, can make Florida feel surprisingly closed despite its reputation for openness.

Sometimes your real estate or financial advisor doubles as your Connector. Sometimes it's someone entirely different; a chamber leader, fellow executive, investor, or local founder who becomes your guide to how things actually work here.

You don't need to chase Connectors. You attract them by demonstrating genuine curiosity, adding value where you can, and showing that you're investing in the community, not just extracting from it.

When people see that you're building something here (not just relocating), they invest back.

WHAT MAKES EXECUTIVE RELOCATION DIFFERENT

Here's what most real estate professionals in Florida don't understand:

executive relocations have completely different requirements than typical moves.

A typical buyer needs help finding a home, getting financing, and closing the deal.

An executive relocating needs help with:

Strategic Timing

- Coordinating move dates with equity vesting schedules
- Understanding how bonus timing affects purchase decisions
- Navigating IPO lockup periods or acquisition scenarios
- Structuring purchases to optimize tax treatment

Domicile Complexity

- Ensuring every step supports future domicile audits
- Coordinating with CPAs on documentation requirements
- Understanding the difference between "moving" and "establishing domicile"
- Avoiding mistakes that create exposure years later

Network Building

- Introductions to other executives in their industry
- Connection to professional organizations that matter
- Understanding where the actual business community operates (not the tourist areas)
- Access to deal flow, investment opportunities, and peer community

Multi-Property Strategy

- Thinking about Anchor, Growth, and Freedom layers simultaneously
- Understanding investment property potential across Florida markets

- Coordinating property portfolio with overall wealth strategy
- Insurance and entity structuring for multiple properties

Confidentiality

- Discretion around employment changes or liquidity events
- Managing information flow when deals are sensitive
- Handling high-net-worth transactions without drawing unwanted attention

Family Integration

- Understanding school options at the level executives expect
- Connecting spouses to professional communities
- Helping children transition socially
- Building family routines that actually work in a new place

Most agents can handle the first item on that list. Very few can handle all of them. And almost none understand how they all interconnect.

WHY "INSIDER KNOWLEDGE" ACTUALLY MATTERS

Look for advisors with at least a decade in the market. Local market knowledge matters because it reveals patterns that current data doesn't show- which neighborhoods have staying power versus hype, where executive communities are genuinely forming, and how different Florida regions cycle.

BUILDING YOUR FULL ADVISORY TEAM

While real estate is often the most visible part of a relocation, you'll need a coordinated team across multiple disciplines.

Think of your team in categories:

Real Estate Professional

- Your anchor for property strategy and market knowledge
- Should understand executive relocations specifically
- Ideally functions as Agent, Advisor, and Connector simultaneously
- Coordinates with your other advisors on timing and structure

Tax Advisor / CPA

- Florida-experienced, ideally with multi-state expertise
- Understands domicile requirements and documentation
- Can advise on entity structure for property ownership
- Coordinates timing of purchases with income recognition
- Integrates Florida move into overall tax strategy

Attorney

- Florida bar admission essential
- Experience with domicile establishment and defense
- Can handle entity formation (LLCs, trusts, etc.)
- Coordinates with CPA on structure
- Understands estate planning implications of Florida residency

Insurance Broker

- Florida-specific experience critical
- Access to multiple carriers (not captive to one company)
- Understands wind mitigation, flood zones, and coastal issues
- Can handle both personal residence and investment properties
- Provides realistic cost projections before you make purchase decisions

Financial Advisor

- Understands how Florida move affects overall wealth strategy
- Can integrate property portfolio decisions into broader planning
- Coordinates with CPA on tax-efficient structures
- Thinks long-term about how your Florida assets fit your goals

Property Manager (if applicable)

- Essential if you're building a Growth property portfolio
- Licensed and insured in Florida
- Experience with your specific property type (long-term vs. short-term rentals)
- Transparent financial reporting
- Established maintenance network

HOW EFFECTIVE EXECUTIVE ADVISORS WORK

Effective executive advisors start with strategic planning before property search, coordinate with your full advisory team (CPA, attorney, financial advisor), provide market education based on your specific criteria, facilitate strategic network introductions, and maintain relationships beyond closing.

HOW TO EVALUATE CHEMISTRY, NOT JUST CREDENTIALS

Every advisor has a resume. Few have chemistry with you specifically.

You're not looking for someone to impress you with credentials. You're looking for someone who understands you, communicates in your language, and shares your values around how relationships should work.

Chemistry shows up in communication style:

- Do they listen carefully before offering solutions?
- Do they challenge your assumptions respectfully when needed?
- Do they follow up promptly and clearly?
- Do they anticipate your questions before you ask them?
- Do they make you feel heard or just "processed"?

Credentials matter: experience, designations, awards, references. But chemistry determines trust. And trust determines whether you'll actually follow their advice when it matters.

In your professional life, you wouldn't hire a VP based solely on their resume. You'd hire them for fit, for how they think, for how they'll work with your existing team. Apply that same instinct here.

An advisor who shares your communication rhythm and values will reduce your stress more than one who simply shares your zip code or price range.

THE QUESTIONS TO ASK

When interviewing potential advisors, ask questions that reveal how they think, not just what they know:

For Real Estate Professionals:

- How many executive relocations have you guided in Florida?
- What's one common mistake you see executives make when they move here?
- How do you coordinate with CPAs and attorneys on timing and structure?
- Can you give me an example of a time you advised a client to wait rather than buy?
- Who else should I be talking to before I make my decision?
- How do you help clients build their professional network here?

For CPAs/Tax Advisors:

- How many Florida domicile cases have you handled?
- What's your experience with domicile audits?
- How do you document and track domicile requirements for clients?
- How do you coordinate with real estate advisors on timing?
- What's your approach to entity structure for property ownership?

For Attorneys:

- How many Florida domicile establishments have you done?
- Have you defended any domicile audits? What was the outcome?
- How do you work with CPAs on coordinated strategy?
- What's your approach to estate planning for new Florida residents?
- How do you handle entity formation for property portfolios?

For All Advisors:

- How do you prefer to communicate during complex transactions?
- What's your philosophy on coordination with other advisors?
- How do you charge for your services?
- What should I expect in terms of time commitment from me?
- Can you provide references from executives you've worked with?

Good advisors answer with insight and specific examples. Great ones turn questions back on you to clarify your priorities before giving advice.

RED FLAGS TO WATCH FOR

As you build your advisory team, watch for these warning signs:

1. **They talk more about themselves than your goals**
2. **They dismiss your concerns or rush through important details**
3. **They avoid or resist coordination with other professionals**
4. **They pressure you into timelines that serve their interests**
5. **They use one-size-fits-all advice for obviously unique situations**
6. **They can't provide references from similar clients**
7. **They're vague about fees or how they get compensated**
8. **They don't ask many questions about your specific situation**
9. **They promise things that sound too good to be true**
10. **Your gut tells you something feels off**

The best professionals in Florida are relationship-driven and long-term focused. If you feel rushed, misaligned, pressured, or unheard, move on quickly. There are plenty of excellent advisors who will treat you as a partner, not a transaction.

THE COMPOUND EFFECT OF THE RIGHT TEAM

When you assemble the right advisory team: people who understand your world, communicate clearly, coordinate effectively, and genuinely care about your long-term success, something remarkable happens.

Decisions get faster. Risks shrink. Opportunities appear that you wouldn't have seen otherwise.

You no longer carry the full mental load of the move alone. You delegate with confidence because everyone around you shares your vision and speaks the same language.

That's the invisible dividend of a well-chosen team, not just smoother transactions, but genuine peace of mind. You can focus on your work, your family, and building your new life, while your advisors handle the complexity.

That's what executive relocation should feel like.

ACTION PLAN: BUILDING YOUR ADVISORY TEAM

1. Assess Your Advisor Needs (30 minutes)

Create a matrix of the advisor roles you need:

- Real Estate Professional
- Tax Advisor/CPA
- Attorney
- Insurance Broker
- Financial Advisor
- Property Manager (if applicable)

For each role, note:

- Critical requirements (what they must have)
- Nice-to-have qualities
- Deal-breakers (what would disqualify them)

Success metric: You have clarity on what you're looking for before you start interviewing.

2. Source Candidates Through Your Network (1-2 weeks)

Ask other executives who've relocated to Florida for recommendations. Specifically ask:

- Who helped you most during your relocation?
- What made them effective?
- What would you do differently in choosing advisors?
- Are there advisors you'd avoid?

Also consider:

- Professional associations in your industry
- Executive forums or peer groups
- CPAs or attorneys you already work with (for Florida referrals)

Success metric: You have 2-3 candidates for each advisor role, sourced through trusted referrals.

3. Conduct Strategic Interviews (2-3 weeks)

For each advisor candidate, schedule a substantive conversation (30-60 minutes). Use the question frameworks provided earlier in this chapter.

Focus on:

- How they think, not just what they know
- How they communicate and coordinate
- Chemistry and values alignment
- Specific experience with situations like yours

Success metric: After interviews, you can clearly articulate why you'd choose (or not choose) each candidate.

4. Check References Thoroughly (1 week)

For your top candidates, ask for references from executives they've worked with on relocations. Ask references:

- What was their situation?
- How did this advisor help them?
- What did they do particularly well?
- What would they have wanted them to do differently?
- Would they work with them again?
- Would they recommend them to other executives?

Success metric: You've spoken with at least 2 references for each advisor you're seriously considering.

5. Build a Shared Communication Framework (1-2 hours)

Once you've selected your advisory team, establish how they'll coordinate:

- Create a shared contact list of all advisors
- Set expectations for communication cadence
- Establish a primary point of coordination (often the real estate advisor or CPA)
- Define decision-making protocols
- Clarify fee structures and payment expectations

Success metric: Your advisors know each other, understand their roles, and have clear coordination protocols.

6. Schedule a Team Kickoff (1 hour)

Bring your key advisors together (conference call or in-person if possible) to:

- Share your goals and timeline
- Review your situation comprehensively
- Identify interdependencies and coordination needs
- Establish milestones and checkpoints
- Surface any concerns or conflicts early

Success metric: Everyone on your team understands the full picture and their role in your success.

7. Create a Decision Matrix for Major Choices (ongoing)

For significant decisions during your relocation, use a simple framework:

- What's the decision to be made?
- Which advisors need to weigh in?
- What's the timeline?
- What are the implications of different choices?
- What's the coordinated recommendation?

Success metric: Major decisions are made strategically with appropriate input, not reactively.

8. Conduct Quarterly Advisor Reviews (15 minutes per quarter)

After you've moved, periodically assess your advisory team:

- Is each advisor still the right fit for current needs?
- Are there gaps in your advisory coverage?
- Should you add or change any advisors?
- Are your advisors coordinating effectively?
- Do you need different expertise for your next phase?

Success metric: Your advisory team evolves as your Florida life evolves.

Coming Up Next

In the next chapter, we'll shift from building your team to building your operational systems. **The Set-Up Stack** will show you how to move from "I live here" to "I operate here". Establishing your identity, entity structure, financial systems, risk management, and workspace in Florida.

But first, complete your advisor selection process. Because the quality of your team determines the quality of everything else.

As I tell every executive: you wouldn't launch a new business unit without the right team. Don't relocate to Florida without one either.

THE SET-UP STACK

FROM MOVED TO OPERATING

THE MOVE IS COMPLETE. The boxes are gone. The palm trees outside your window are real now, not a screensaver.

This is the part no one prepares you for: the quiet space between "I live here" and "I operate here."

For most executives, the transition doesn't fail on motivation. It fails on structure. They move their life but forget to move their systems. Their paperwork still points north, their accounts are scattered, and their new routines never quite click.

Relocation isn't finished until your life runs smoothly again. That's what the **Set-Up Stack** is for. A framework to rebuild your personal and professional operating system.

From watching executives settle into Florida, I can tell you: the ones who integrate fastest treat this phase like a product launch. They have checklists, timelines, and accountability. The ones who struggle think "it will all work itself out eventually."

It won't. You have to build it.

WHY SYSTEMS MATTER MORE THAN SCENERY

After any big move, there's a temptation to relax. You've made it through the logistics, the closing, and the relocation grind. But this stage is where stability takes shape.

Think of this as the post-launch phase of a new business unit. You're live, but the processes aren't mature yet.

Your goal now is consistency. To remove friction, create clarity, and give yourself the infrastructure to thrive.

The Set-Up Stack has six layers: **Identity, Entity, Money, Risk, Team, and Workspace.**

Layer 1: Identity

Identity is the foundation of your new operating system. It's how the world recognizes you, both legally and professionally.

Start with the obvious: driver's license, voter registration, mailing address, and professional memberships. Update them everywhere: banks, insurers, the IRS, and every account tied to your name.

Then move to your digital footprint. Update your website, email signatures, and social profiles to reflect your new base of operations. People associate presence with credibility. If you're building a network in Florida but your LinkedIn still says "Boston," you're signaling that the move is temporary.

Identity alignment is more than paperwork. It's reputation management. When your public, legal, and personal records all point to the same place, you send a powerful message: *I'm here to stay.*

THE 30-DAY IDENTITY SPRINT

Week 1:

- Florida driver's license (surrender old state license at DMV)
- Voter registration
- Vehicle registration and title transfer
- Declaration of Domicile filed with county clerk

Week 2:

- USPS permanent address change
- Update address with IRS (Form 8822)
- Update all insurance policies (auto, home, life, health)
- Notify employer of address change

Week 3:

- Update all bank accounts, credit cards, investment accounts
- Change address on all professional licenses
- Update professional association memberships
- Revise email signature and LinkedIn profile

Week 4:

- Update company/entity filings with new address
- Change address on any recurring subscriptions
- Update emergency contacts for family members
- Final sweep: check for any remaining old-state addresses

By day 30, your identity should be cleanly Florida-based everywhere that matters.

Layer 2: Entity

For executives, founders, and consultants, this is where structure gets serious.

If you have an LLC, corporation, or trust based in another state, review how your move affects it. You may need to register a new entity, update addresses, or create subsidiary structures.

Florida is business-friendly, but that doesn't mean every filing is automatic. Talk with your attorney or CPA about how domicile impacts ownership, payroll, and taxation.

The principle is simple: your entity should live where you live.

COMMON ENTITY SCENARIOS

Scenario 1: You Own a Single-Member LLC in Your Old State

Action: File a foreign qualification to operate in Florida, or dissolve and re-form as Florida LLC. Update registered agent address to Florida.

Why it matters: Entity location affects where you file taxes, where you're subject to legal jurisdiction, and how your domicile is perceived.

Scenario 2: You're a Founder with a Delaware C-Corp

Action: The corporation can stay in Delaware (common for VC-backed companies), but update your personal address on all corporate documents. File annual reports showing Florida address for officers/directors.

Why it matters: Your domicile is separate from company domicile, but consistency across documents strengthens your proof stack.

Scenario 3: You Have Multiple Entities (Operating Company + Holding Company)

Action: Work with your attorney to review structure. May need to establish Florida entities for holdings, real estate, or consulting work.

Why it matters: Proper entity structure protects assets and can optimize tax treatment.

Scenario 4: You're W-2 Employee with No Business Entities

Action: May still want to establish a Florida LLC for future consulting, board work, or real estate holdings.

Why it matters: Creates optionality for future income streams and asset protection.

Having the right structure gives you flexibility. It lets you separate assets, simplify accounting, and protect what you've built.

Treat this step like corporate housekeeping, Not glamorous, but essential for long-term control.

Layer 3: Money

Money flow is where stability becomes visible.

Open local banking relationships early. Build a connection with a community or regional bank in addition to any national institutions you use. Local bankers can become valuable connectors, they know who's building what.

THE FINANCIAL INFRASTRUCTURE REBUILD

Banking:

- Open primary checking/savings at Florida-based bank or credit union
- Maintain national bank if needed, but establish local presence
- Update direct deposit addresses with employers
- Set up bill pay from Florida accounts

Credit:

- Update billing addresses on all credit cards
- Review credit report to ensure address is updated
- Notify credit bureaus of address change
- Check that credit inquiries show Florida address

Investments:

- Update brokerage account addresses
- Review beneficiary designations (may need to update under Florida law)
- Confirm that statements mail to Florida address
- Discuss any entity changes with financial advisor

Insurance:

- Transfer all policies to Florida address (auto, home, life, health, umbrella)
- Shop for better rates with Florida-based insurers
- Update beneficiaries if needed
- Confirm coverage amounts still make sense

Payroll and Benefits:

- Update W-4 to reflect Florida address
- Review 401(k) and HSA addresses
- Update beneficiaries on all employer benefits
- Confirm health insurance network includes Florida providers

Consider how your relocation changes cash flow rhythm. Property taxes, utilities, and insurance schedules may operate on different cycles. Sync them into your financial dashboard so you always see a full picture.

Finally, revisit your investment and retirement allocations. Florida's cost of living, tax profile, and investment opportunities differ from your previous state. Align your portfolio with your new reality.

Money moves best when it has a clear path. Build that path deliberately.

Layer 4: Risk

Risk management is often the last thing people think about, and the first thing they regret ignoring.

Relocation introduces new types of risk: environmental, legal, and financial.

THE RISK AUDIT

Property Risk:

- Review wind, flood, and liability coverage with Florida-based broker
- Understand what your policy covers (and excludes) for hurricanes, flooding
- Get flood insurance if in flood zone (even if not required by lender)
- Consider umbrella policy for additional liability protection
- Document all personal property (photos, receipts) for insurance claims

Personal Risk:

- Update estate plan to reflect Florida law
- Review and re-execute will under Florida jurisdiction
- Update powers of attorney (financial and healthcare)
- Revise healthcare directives / living wills
- Review and update all beneficiary designations

Financial Risk:

- Ensure assets are properly titled (individual, joint, trust)
- Review whether trusts need to be re-domiciled or amended
- Check that business liabilities are contained within proper entities

- Consider asset protection strategies (Florida has strong homestead protection)

Identity Risk:

- Update security questions that reference old state information
- Enable two-factor authentication on all financial accounts
- Monitor credit reports quarterly for address-related fraud
- Update password manager with new address information

Continuity Risk:

- Identify who can act on your behalf if you travel or face emergency
- Update emergency contact information with all providers
- Share key document locations with trusted family member or attorney
- Consider whether you need local trustee or executor

Risk is never eliminated, only managed. The goal is not fear but foresight.

Layer 5: Team

Your team isn't just your professional network. It's everyone who helps you live efficiently.

Start with core professionals: accountant, attorney, insurance broker, financial planner. Then layer in the everyday support that keeps your life moving: contractors, healthcare providers, and service vendors.

BUILDING YOUR FLORIDA SUPPORT TEAM

Professional Core:

- **CPA/Tax Advisor:** Must understand multi-state issues and Florida tax advantages

- **Attorney:** Florida-licensed for estate planning, real estate, business matters
- **Insurance Broker:** Local expertise in property, auto, umbrella policies
- **Financial Advisor:** Can integrate Florida-specific strategies (no state income tax means different planning)

Healthcare:

- Primary care physician
- Dentist
- Any specialists you see regularly
- Veterinarian (if you have pets)
- Pharmacy (transfer prescriptions)

Property and Home:

- General contractor or handyman
- HVAC specialist (critical in Florida)
- Pool service (if applicable)
- Lawn care
- Pest control (more important in Florida than many northern states)

Personal Services:

- Hair salon/barber
- Dry cleaner
- Auto mechanic
- Gym or fitness studio

Many executives forget to rebuild this part of the ecosystem. They rely on old relationships from another state, which slows down decision-making.

Create a contact list of trusted local providers and keep it current.

FAMILY LOGISTICS

This is also where family setup fits:

For Families with Kids:

- Enroll in schools (deadlines vary by district)
- Find pediatrician
- Identify extracurricular activities (sports, music, etc.)
- Connect with other families in neighborhood/school
- Update school records with Florida address and contacts

For Everyone:

- Find religious/spiritual community (if applicable)
- Identify local recreation opportunities
- Locate nearest hospital/urgent care
- Join community groups or social organizations
- Establish regular routines (grocery store, coffee shop, etc.)

The faster these rhythms stabilize, the sooner your new life feels normal.

A well-built team makes Florida feel less like a relocation and more like an upgrade.

Layer 6: Workspace

Where you work influences how you work.

Whether you're fully remote, hybrid, or still commuting to an office, your physical workspace sets the tone for performance.

DESIGNING YOUR FLORIDA WORKSPACE

Home Office Setup:

- Dedicated workspace with good natural light
- Ergonomic furniture (desk, chair)

- Reliable high-speed internet (test speeds, may need upgrade)
- Backup power (power outages happen during storms - consider UPS)
- Proper climate control (AC is critical year-round)
- Video call background (professional or blurred)

Technology Infrastructure:

- Mesh WiFi system if large home
- Separate work network if needed for security
- Cloud backup for all critical files
- VPN access if required by employer
- Quality webcam and microphone for remote meetings

Co-working Options:

- Research local co-working spaces for variety
- Day passes for coffee shop working
- Hotel lobbies or libraries for quiet focus time
- Professional meeting spaces for client meetings

Outdoor Workspace Opportunities (Florida advantage):

- Screened porch or patio workspace
- Backyard office shed
- Pool deck for reading/thinking time
- Beach or park for walking meetings

Workspace isn't just physical. It's psychological. Having a defined place to create and lead reinforces your sense of purpose.

The best relocations aren't escapes from work; they're redesigns of how work fits into life.

Florida's climate allows for flexibility: outdoor meetings, quiet mornings on the patio, or creative breaks near the water. Use that advantage.

BRINGING THE STACK TOGETHER

The Set-Up Stack is less about paperwork and more about alignment.

When your identity, entity, finances, risk plan, team, and workspace all point in the same direction, you create operational harmony. Decisions get easier because your systems support them.

This alignment gives you leverage. You spend less time managing life and more time living it.

Executives who master this stage often say the same thing: "It finally feels real." That's the moment your relocation stops being a project and starts being a platform.

THE STORY OF AARON

Aaron was a Chief Technology Officer from Seattle who moved to Naples. He had planned everything; the home, the timing, the finances. But six months in, he felt scattered.

His company mail still went to Washington. His LLC was registered in Delaware with Washington mailing address. His doctor was still back home via telemedicine. Every small task required extra effort.

After a frustrating tax season, he decided to rebuild systematically. Within 90 days, he updated all addresses, re-domiciled his LLC to Florida, found local professionals (CPA, attorney, doctor), and converted a spare room to a proper office with upgraded internet. Everything synced. His mornings felt lighter. His workday started earlier. The move finally "clicked."

That's the power of systems alignment. It doesn't make your life different; it makes your life easier.

THE 90-DAY SET-UP TIMELINE

Let me give you a realistic timeline for completing your Set-Up Stack:

Days 1-30: Foundation (Identity + Entity)

Week 1:

- Move in, unpack essentials
- File Declaration of Domicile
- Get Florida driver's license
- Register to vote

Week 2:

- Register vehicles
- Update insurance policies
- Set up USPS forwarding

Week 3:

- Open Florida bank account
- Update employer address
- Begin updating financial accounts

Week 4:

- Meet with Florida CPA and attorney
- Discuss entity needs
- Update all professional memberships

Success metric: Core identity documents reflect Florida by day 30.

Days 31-60: Infrastructure (Money + Risk)

Week 5:

- Complete all banking transitions
- Transfer investment account addresses
- Update credit cards and billing

Week 6:

- Estate planning consultation
- Update will, POA, healthcare directives
- Review all insurance coverage

Week 7:

- File entity registrations if needed
- Update business documents
- Review asset titling

Week 8:

- Conduct comprehensive risk audit
- Ensure all beneficiaries updated
- Create password/document inventory

Success metric: All financial and legal infrastructure points to Florida by day 60.

Days 61-90: Integration (Team + Workspace)

Week 9:

- Establish healthcare providers
- Find home service vendors
- Set up routine service schedules

Week 10:

- Optimize workspace setup
- Test all technology infrastructure
- Join local professional groups

Week 11:

- Complete family integration (schools, activities)
- Establish social routines
- Build emergency contact list

Week 12:

- Conduct full systems review
- Identify any remaining gaps
- Celebrate successful integration

Success metric: Life runs smoothly without constant problem-solving by day 90.

THE LONG-TERM PAYOFF

The executives who thrive after relocation all share a common trait: operational discipline.

They treat their lives like organizations: clear processes, clear accountability, and clear rhythms. That doesn't mean rigid schedules or corporate spreadsheets at home. It means consistency.

When you bring that same professionalism to your personal life, you gain freedom. You trust that the details are handled, so your energy goes where it matters.

The Set-Up Stack is a blueprint for independence. Once it's in place, you'll never have to think about "settling in" again. You'll already be operating.

WHY THIS PHASE MATTERS FOR YOUR LONG-TERM SUCCESS

I've watched many executives move to Florida over the years. The correlation is clear:

Executives who complete their Set-Up Stack within 90 days:

- Integrate into business community 3-5x faster
- Report higher satisfaction after 1 year
- Make fewer "I should have done this sooner" mistakes
- Build wealth more effectively (better advisors, better decisions)

Executives who let it drag out for 6-12 months:

- Struggle with scattered systems and constant friction
- Miss business opportunities due to incomplete setup
- Pay "stupid tax" on preventable mistakes
- Often consider moving again because "it's not working"

The difference isn't talent or resources. It's systematic execution.

ACTION PLAN: BUILDING YOUR SET-UP STACK

1. Create Your Master Set-Up Checklist (2 hours)

Exercise: Build a comprehensive checklist of every system that needs updating.

Use this structure:

Identity:

- Florida driver's license
- Voter registration
- Vehicle registration
- Professional memberships
- LinkedIn/online profiles
- [Add all your specific items]

Entity:

- Review current entity structure with attorney
- File foreign qualification or new Florida entity

- Update registered agent addresses
- [Add your specific items]

Money:

- Open Florida bank account
- Update all investment accounts
- Transfer insurance policies
- [Add all your specific items]

Risk:

- Meet with Florida estate attorney
- Update will, POA, healthcare directives
- Review all insurance coverage
- [Add your specific items]

Team:

- Find Florida CPA
- Find Florida attorney
- Establish healthcare providers
- [Add all your specific providers]

Workspace:

- Set up home office
- Upgrade internet if needed
- Research co-working options
- [Add your specific needs]

Success metric: You have a complete checklist with 50-75 items across all six layers.

2. Assign Deadlines to Every Item (1 hour)

Exercise: Next to each checklist item, add a realistic deadline.

Use the 90-day framework:

- Days 1-30: Identity + Entity (foundation)
- Days 31-60: Money + Risk (infrastructure)
- Days 61-90: Team + Workspace (integration)

Be realistic but firm. "Someday" items never get done.

Success metric: Every item has a specific deadline.

3. Identify Your "Must Do Immediately" Items (30 minutes)

Exercise: From your master checklist, flag the 10 items that must be done in the first 7 days.

These are typically:

- Driver's license
- Vehicle registration
- Declaration of domicile
- Voter registration
- Insurance transfers
- USPS forwarding
- Employer address update
- Bank account opening
- [Your critical items]

Success metric: You know exactly what MUST be done in week one.

4. Build Your Professional Team List (2 hours)

Exercise: Research and shortlist professionals you'll need:

For each professional category, identify 2-3 candidates:

Florida CPA specializing in executive relocations:

- Candidate 1: [Name, firm, referral source]
- Candidate 2: [Name, firm, referral source]

Florida estate attorney:

- Candidate 1: [Name, firm, referral source]
- Candidate 2: [Name, firm, referral source]

Insurance broker (property, auto, umbrella):

- Candidate 1: [Name, firm, referral source]
- Candidate 2: [Name, firm, referral source]

Primary care physician:

- Candidate 1: [Name, practice, insurance accepted]
- Candidate 2: [Name, practice, insurance accepted]

Success metric: You have specific names to contact, not just "I'll find someone later."

5. Schedule Your Coordination Call (immediate)

Exercise: Within your first 30 days, schedule one coordination call with your core advisory team:

Attendees:

- You (and spouse if applicable)
- Florida CPA
- Florida attorney
- Your real estate advisor (if they helped coordinate the move)

Agenda:

- Review your Set-Up Stack plan
- Clarify who owns which items
- Identify any gaps or dependencies
- Set 60-day and 90-day check-in dates

Success metric: Everyone is aligned on the plan and their role in it.

6. Create Your Florida Document Repository (1 hour)

Exercise: Set up a secure digital folder (or physical binder) for all Florida documents.

BONUS: this can be a big help during Hurricane season. These docs should all be on a thumb drive and hardcopy and go into your Go-Bag in case of an evacuation.

Structure:

- Identity (driver's license copy, voter registration, vehicle registrations)
- Entity (formation docs, registered agent confirmations, annual reports)
- Money (bank account info, investment statements, insurance policies)
- Risk (will, POA, healthcare directives, insurance policies)
- Team (contact list with all providers)
- Property (deed, survey, inspection reports, insurance, HOA docs)

Success metric: You can find any critical document in under 2 minutes. (Like if there is a Hurricane evacuation, see above)

7. Conduct 30-60-90 Day Reviews (recurring)

Exercise: Schedule three review sessions on your calendar:

Day 30 Review:

- What's complete from the checklist?
- What's delayed and why?
- What problems emerged that weren't anticipated?
- Adjust timeline for remaining items

Day 60 Review:

- Infrastructure complete?
- Any system integration issues?
- Team members all in place?
- Workspace functional?

Day 90 Review:

- Full Set-Up Stack operational?
- Life running smoothly?
- What would you do differently?
- What advice would you give someone starting now?

Success metric: You have calendar holds for all three reviews.

8. The "Smooth Operations Test" (Day 90)

Exercise: On day 90, ask yourself these questions:

- Can I handle a business emergency without scrambling for information?
- Do I know who to call for any household issue?
- Are all my legal and financial systems Florida-based?
- Does my workspace support my best work?
- Have I established regular routines?
- Do I feel settled, not scattered?

If you answer "yes" to 5 of 6, your Set-Up Stack is solid.

If you answer "no" to 3 or more, extend your timeline and address gaps.

Coming Up

In the final chapter, we'll discuss **Designing Your New Life (Freedom Metrics)**. How to measure success not in dollars saved, but in freedom earned. We'll show you how to create sustainable rhythms that compound quality of life over decades.

But first, complete your Set-Up Stack exercises. Because operational systems aren't glamorous, but they're what separate executives who thrive from executives who survive.

As I tell every executive: infrastructure is invisible until it's missing. Build it properly once, and you'll benefit from it for years.

DESIGNING YOUR NEW LIFE (FREEDOM METRICS)

BEYOND RELOCATION TO REINVENTION

EVERY EXECUTIVE who relocates has a moment when they stop and ask, "Did it work?"

The numbers look good. The taxes are lower, the view is better, and the stress is different. But success after a move isn't measured in spreadsheets. It's measured in space. The space between meetings, between obligations, between who you were before and who you're becoming now.

Relocation gives you an opportunity that few people ever get: a blank operating system. The challenge is deciding what to run on it.

I call this the phase of *designing your new life.* You've optimized the inputs. Where you live, how you work, who you're surrounded by, but now you get to define the outputs. What kind of life are you building with all this freedom you just earned?

To answer that, I use a simple framework: **The Freedom Metrics.**

These Freedom Metrics are how you measure the Lifestyle ROI component we discussed in Chapter 2. While Financial ROI tracks the money you keep, Lifestyle ROI, measured through these three metrics, tracks the life you gain.

From watching executives navigate this transition, I've learned that freedom isn't a feeling. It's a system. And like any system, it can be measured, managed, and optimized.

THE FREEDOM METRICS

Freedom has three dimensions: **Time, Health, and Contribution.**

Together, they form the ultimate return on relocation. They're not about luxury or leisure. They're about control.

When you design around these three, you stop chasing balance and start creating alignment.

1. Time: The Currency of Control

The first and most important Freedom Metric is time. How much of it you own and how you use it.

Time is the one resource you can't earn back. You can leverage money, delegate tasks, and outsource work, but you can't create more hours. What relocation gives you, if you use it wisely, is control over the distribution of those hours.

Executives often underestimate how much time they've been giving away. Commutes, meetings, obligations that exist out of habit rather than necessity. Florida's rhythm forces you to look at your calendar differently. The pace invites reflection.

Here's a simple test: open your calendar and color-code the entries. Green for energy-giving activities. Red for energy-draining ones.

How does it look?

Freedom begins when the greens start to outnumber the reds.

Use your time as a design tool. Protect your mornings for creative or strategic work. Cluster meetings. Leave space for movement, rest, and family. You've built a system that runs efficiently. Now give it room to breathe.

Owning your time isn't about doing less. It's about doing what matters.

What this looks like in practice:

When I first moved to Florida, my calendar looked like my calendar "back home"; back-to-back meetings, reactive scheduling, no white space. It took me six months to realize I'd moved geography but not rhythm.

The breakthrough came when I started blocking my mornings for strategic thinking and creative work. No meetings before 10 AM. That single change gave me 12-15 hours per week of focused time. My productivity went up, my stress went down, and my decision quality improved dramatically.

That's what owning your time looks like.

2. Health: The Foundation of Sustainability

The second Freedom Metric is health: physical, mental, and emotional.

Executives rarely admit how much performance depends on well-being. We treat health like a variable when it's actually infrastructure. Without it, nothing else scales.

Relocation gives you the environment to rebuild that foundation. Sunshine, fresh air, walkable neighborhoods, water, and community. Florida's natural design invites a healthier rhythm if you let it.

Use it. Walk in the mornings before work. Schedule movement into your calendar like a meeting you can't cancel. Find a local doctor and fitness routine early so you don't drift back into "someday" mode.

Your health is the quiet multiplier behind every other return. It improves focus, patience, creativity, and connection. It's what lets you operate with energy instead of effort.

When people say they feel younger after moving, what they're really saying is that their inputs changed. The environment supports vitality instead of draining it.

What this looks like in practice:

I watch executives arrive in Tampa Bay and immediately transform their health routines. One CTO I know started cycling to coffee meetings instead of driving. Lost 25 pounds in six months without "trying", just changed his daily pattern.

Another executive started paddleboarding before work. Said it gave him two benefits: exercise and forced meditation (can't check email on a paddleboard).

These aren't dramatic interventions. They're environmental advantages. Use them.

3. Contribution: The Currency of Meaning

The third Freedom Metric is contribution: what you give back to the systems that support you.

Relocation isn't just about personal gain. It's also about reinvestment. When you contribute to your new community, you accelerate belonging. You turn a place on the map into a place that matters.

Contribution looks different for everyone. For some, it's mentoring startups or advising young founders. For others, it's volunteering, teaching, or supporting local causes. For a few, it's simply showing up. Being present at community events, supporting small businesses, or helping neighbors.

Whatever form it takes, contribution closes the loop between success and significance.

Executives who thrive here talk about the satisfaction of being part of something again. Not just building companies but building communities. They find joy in giving momentum to others.

That's the ultimate relocation ROI: when your success multiplies beyond yourself.

What this looks like in practice:

I've watched executives go from "too busy for community involvement" to serving on nonprofit boards, mentoring at startup incubators, teaching at local universities, and hosting peer groups.

One CFO I know started a quarterly "Finance Leaders Breakfast" in Tampa. No agenda, no pitches - just peer discussion. It's become one of the most valuable networking groups in the market. He's not doing it for business development. He's doing it because he can.

That's contribution as freedom metric.

FREEDOM AS A SYSTEM, NOT A FEELING

Freedom doesn't happen by accident. It happens by design.

It's the cumulative effect of a thousand small choices. How you schedule, who you hire, what you delegate, and what you decline. It's built through clarity.

Look back at the frameworks you've built throughout this book:

- **Relocation ROI** taught you to measure the value of your move
- **The Proof Stack** protected your foundation
- **The Timing Triad** gave you leverage
- **The Florida Fit Matrix** matched your energy
- **The Network Flywheel** created momentum
- **The Property Portfolio** built wealth and stability
- **The Advisor Spectrum** ensured you had guidance
- **The Set-Up Stack** gave you systems

Each of those frameworks now feeds into this one. They were never separate. They were scaffolding for freedom.

Now it's time to run the system.

THE STORY OF DANIEL

Daniel was a Chief Revenue Officer who relocated from New York to Tampa. His move was flawless. Domicile filed, taxes optimized, team relocated. On paper, everything was perfect. But after six months, he felt restless.

The work was fine. The house was beautiful. Yet something was missing. He described it as "a quiet hum of dissatisfaction."

When we talked, I asked him what his calendar looked like. He laughed. "Exactly like it did before. Just with palm trees outside the window."

That was the problem. He'd moved geography but not design.

We built his Freedom Metrics together. He set clear non-negotiables:

- Daily exercise (non-negotiable morning routine)
- Two uninterrupted evenings a week with family
- One morning reserved for strategic thinking and creative work
- Contribution goal: mentor two early-stage founders per quarter

He joined Tampa Bay Technology Forum and started mentoring early-stage founders. Within three months, his calendar looked different. His energy felt different.

He told me: "I finally feel like I moved."

Freedom isn't where you live. It's how you live when you get there.

DESIGNING YOUR OPERATING WEEK

One of the most practical ways to measure your Freedom Metrics is through your weekly design.

The Weekly Freedom Audit

1. Time Audit: Track where your hours go for one week. Identify what can be automated, delegated, or deleted.

2. Energy Audit: Note when you feel most focused or drained. Adjust your schedule to match your energy curve.

3. Freedom Block: Reserve two to three recurring windows each week for activities that restore you: family time, learning, reflection, or recreation. Treat them as immovable.

4. Contribution Block: Schedule time to mentor, volunteer, or support a community initiative. You'll be surprised how much energy giving creates.

This isn't about rigid scheduling. It's about conscious design. When your calendar reflects your values, you stop managing time and start living it.

My weekly rhythm (example):

After 30 years of iterating, here's what works for me:

Mondays: Strategic planning morning (7-10 AM), client work afternoon, networking event evening (once or twice per month)

Tuesdays-Thursdays: Client-facing work, meetings, active productivity

Fridays: Wrap-up morning, lunch with peer or mentee, afternoon personal time

Weekends: Family, recreation, reading, no scheduled work

Daily constants: Morning walk (6:30 AM), no meetings before 9 AM, dinner with family

This rhythm gives me predictability (I know what each day is for) and flexibility (I can move things within reason).

Your rhythm will differ based on your role, family situation, and personality. The point is to design it intentionally.

MEASURING THE INTANGIBLES

You can't put freedom on a balance sheet, but you can sense it in patterns.

Ask yourself:

- Do I feel calm when I start the day?
- Do I end most weeks proud of how I spent my time?
- Am I building health and relationships instead of depleting them?
- Do I feel connected to my community?
- Am I making progress on things that matter to me personally, not just professionally?

If the answers lean yes more often than no, your system is working.

Freedom is an internal KPI. You feel it before you can explain it.

THE QUARTERLY FREEDOM REVIEW

Every 90 days, ask yourself:

Time:

- How much of my calendar do I actually control?
- What percentage of my time goes to energy-giving vs. energy-draining activities?
- Where am I still giving away time unnecessarily?

Health:

- Am I moving my body regularly?
- Am I sleeping well?
- Do I have energy for what matters?
- When was my last full physical checkup?

Contribution:

- What have I given to my community this quarter?
- Who have I helped?
- Where have I added value beyond my job?

These simple check-ins keep you honest about whether you're maintaining freedom or letting it erode.

THE ART OF MAINTENANCE

Freedom isn't permanent. It's maintained.

The same way you review financials each quarter, review your Freedom Metrics. Are you slipping back into old habits? Are new obligations creeping in?

The beauty of Florida's environment is that it constantly reminds you of what matters. The weather, the light, the space. They all nudge you to slow down and recalibrate. Use that reminder.

Your new life doesn't need to be perfect. It just needs to be intentional.

WARNING SIGNS THAT FREEDOM IS ERODING:

- Your calendar is filling up with obligations you don't remember agreeing to
- You're working more hours than you did before the move
- You haven't exercised or spent time outdoors in weeks
- You can't remember the last time you had a meal without checking your phone
- You're saying "yes" to things because you feel guilty saying "no"
- You're not making time for contribution or community

If you see three or more of these, it's time to recalibrate.

THE RIPPLE EFFECT

When you live with clarity, everyone around you benefits. Teams become calmer. Families feel more connected. Opportunities start aligning with your priorities instead of distracting from them.

Executives who design for freedom often find their companies improve too. They make better decisions because their minds aren't crowded with noise. They communicate more clearly because they're living in sync with what they believe.

That's the quiet power of relocation. It's not the sunshine that changes you. It's the simplicity.

The compound effect over time:

Year 1: You notice the time savings and lower stress

Year 2: You notice the health improvements and energy increase

Year 3: You notice the contribution and community connections

Year 5: You realize you've built a completely different life

Year 10: You can't imagine having stayed where you were

The ROI compounds in ways that aren't immediately visible but become undeniable over time.

WHY THIS CHAPTER MATTERS FOR YOUR RELOCATION SUCCESS

I've watched hundreds of executives move to Florida over three decades. The ones who struggle most aren't the ones who picked the wrong house or market. They're the ones who moved their location but not their life design.

They recreated the same calendar, the same stress patterns, the same trade-offs in a different zip code. The palm trees looked nice, but nothing fundamental changed.

The executives who thrive are the ones who treat relocation as a reset opportunity. They redesign how they work, when they work, what they commit to, and what they protect.

That's what this chapter is about: using relocation as a catalyst for systematic life improvement, not just geographic change.

Action Plan: Designing Freedom

Complete these exercises to measure and optimize your freedom:

1. Define Your Personal Freedom Metrics (1 hour)

Exercise: Write your own definitions of the three Freedom Metrics in your own words.

Time: What does "owning my time" mean to me specifically?

Example: "I control 70%+ of my calendar. No more than 3 meetings per day. Mornings protected for deep work."

Health: What does "maintaining health" mean to me specifically?

Example: "Exercise 4x per week. 7+ hours sleep nightly. Annual physical. Stress level manageable."

Contribution: What does "meaningful contribution" look like for me?

Example: "Mentor 2 founders per quarter. Serve on one nonprofit board. Host peer group monthly."

Success metric: You can explain what freedom looks like in concrete, measurable terms.

2. The Calendar Color-Code Exercise (30 minutes)

Exercise: Review your last two weeks of calendar. Color-code every entry:

- **Green:** Energy-giving (strategic work, creative projects, meaningful meetings)
- **Yellow:** Neutral (necessary but not energizing)

- **Red:** Energy-draining (obligation meetings, administrative tasks)

Calculate percentages:

- What % of your time is green?
- What % is yellow?
- What % is red?

Target ratios:

- 50%+ green (energy-giving)
- 30-40% yellow (necessary)
- 10-20% red (minimize these)

Success metric: You see clearly where your time goes and can identify opportunities to optimize.

3. Identify One Specific Change Per Metric (45 minutes)

Exercise: For each Freedom Metric, identify one concrete change you'll make in the next 30 days.

Time change: "I will [specific action] to gain [specific amount] of time back."

Example: "I will decline all meetings before 9 AM to gain 5 hours per week of focused morning time."

Health change: "I will [specific action] to improve [specific aspect] of my health."

Example: "I will join a local gym and work out 3x per week before work."

Contribution change: "I will [specific action] to give back to [specific community]."

Example: "I will reach out to Tampa Bay Wave and sign up as a mentor for one startup."

Success metric: You have three specific, actionable commitments.

4. Audit Your Calendar and Reallocate (1 hour)

Exercise: Look at your next month of calendar. Identify opportunities to reallocate time toward what energizes you.

Actions:

- Cancel or decline 2-3 low-value recurring meetings
- Block 2-3 "Freedom Blocks" per week for strategic/creative work
- Add 1 contribution activity to your calendar
- Schedule 1-2 health activities as "meetings" that can't be moved

Success metric: Your calendar for the next month looks noticeably different than the previous month.

5. Commit to One Recurring Practice (immediate)

Exercise: Choose one practice that sustains health and commit to it for 90 days.

Options:

- Morning walk or run before work
- Gym or fitness class 3x per week
- Paddleboarding or cycling on weekends
- Yoga or meditation daily
- Tennis or pickleball twice weekly

Success metric: You have a recurring calendar hold and you've told someone about your commitment (accountability).

6. Join or Support One Community Initiative (within 60 days)

Exercise: Select one way to contribute meaningfully to your Florida community.

Options:

- Mentor at startup incubator (Wave, accelerators)
- Join nonprofit board or volunteer regularly
- Start a peer group (breakfast series, roundtable)
- Guest lecture at local university
- Host networking events at your home

Success metric: You've made contact and scheduled your first contribution activity.

7. Reassess Your Freedom Metrics Quarterly (recurring)

Exercise: Every 90 days, review your three Freedom Metrics:

Questions to ask:

Time:

- Am I owning more or less of my calendar than 90 days ago?
- What's taking time that shouldn't be?
- Where have I created new space?

Health:

- Am I moving more or less than 90 days ago?
- How's my energy level?
- What needs attention?

Contribution:

- What have I given back this quarter?
- Where have I made an impact?
- What's next?

Success metric: You have quarterly calendar holds for these reviews and you actually do them.

8. The "Freedom Portfolio" Exercise (ongoing)

Exercise: Create a simple document tracking your freedom progress over time.

Structure:

Month 1:

- Time: [observations, wins, challenges]
- Health: [observations, wins, challenges]
- Contribution: [observations, wins, challenges]

Month 3:

- Time: [observations, wins, challenges]
- Health: [observations, wins, challenges]
- Contribution: [observations, wins, challenges]

Month 6:

- Time: [observations, wins, challenges]
- Health: [observations, wins, challenges]
- Contribution: [observations, wins, challenges]

Month 12:

- Time: [observations, wins, challenges]
- Health: [observations, wins, challenges]
- Contribution: [observations, wins, challenges]

This creates a narrative of your freedom journey. When you read back through it, you'll see patterns and progress that aren't obvious day-to-day.

Success metric: You have a document that tells the story of your transformation.

THE FINAL WORD ON FREEDOM

If you've built the systems, aligned the calendars, chosen the market, and found your rhythm, then you've already succeeded.

Now the work is to live it. To let the days flow instead of forcing them, to keep refining the design one decision at a time.

You didn't move to slow down. You moved to live intentionally. To work when you choose, rest when you need, and build things that outlast you.

That's the Freedom Dividend. Life that pays you back in time, health, and purpose.

Freedom is not the absence of work. It's the presence of alignment. When your environment, systems, and purpose move in the same direction, life stops feeling busy and starts feeling built.

You didn't move to slow down. You moved to operate differently.

Welcome home.

EPILOGUE: THE FREEDOM DIVIDEND

WHEN PEOPLE ASK what surprised me most about moving to Florida, I tell them it wasn't the sunshine. It was the silence.

For the first time in years, there was space between things.

Space between meetings. Space between thoughts. Space between who I was on the way up and who I was ready to become next.

That silence became clarity. And clarity became freedom.

The longer you live here, the more you realize that the real dividend of relocation isn't money saved or taxes avoided. It's margin. The distance between effort and exhaustion.

Freedom, it turns out, compounds.

What You Built

If you've made it this far, you've done more than change an address. You've built a platform.

- You measured your **Relocation ROI** (Chapter 2), understanding that Financial ROI plus Lifestyle ROI equals total return.

- You proved your **Domicile Proof Stack** (Chapter 3), building the four layers of Intent, Paperwork, Presence, and Patterns.
- You timed your move with the **Timing Triad** (Chapter 4), synchronizing your Personal, Financial, and Legal calendars.
- You chose your place through the **Florida Fit Matrix** (Chapter 5), matching your energy to the right market.
- You built your **Network Flywheel** (Chapter 6), creating momentum through contribution and consistency.
- You structured your **Property Portfolio** (Chapter 7), thinking strategically about Anchor, Growth, and Freedom properties.
- You assembled your **Advisory Team** (Chapter 8), finding the right Agent, Advisor, and Connector support.
- You launched your **Set-Up Stack** (Chapter 9), systematically rebuilding your Identity, Entity, Money, Risk, Team, and Workspace.
- And you designed your **Freedom Metrics** (Chapter 10), measuring success through Time, Health, and Contribution.

Each framework wasn't just a tool; it was training. Together they taught you how to run your life like the kind of company you'd actually want to work for.

Now the company is you.

The reward is not retirement. It's reinvention.

The Dividend Defined

A dividend is the return you get from owning something valuable and managing it well.

In this case, the asset is your time, your energy, and your attention.

The **Freedom Dividend** pays out differently for everyone.

For some, it's a morning without alarm clocks. For others, it's dinner with family that isn't rushed. For a few, it's the chance to build something entirely new without burning out the way they did the first time.

You'll know you're collecting it when work starts feeling lighter again. When ambition stops competing with peace.

The great paradox of relocation is that the more you simplify, the more potential you unlock. Florida gives you room to breathe, and in that oxygen, ideas expand.

The Next Chapter

The longer you live here, the more you notice a quiet rhythm. The days start earlier, the evenings stretch longer, and life feels less like a sprint and more like a sequence.

That rhythm invites creativity. Many executives end up writing again, mentoring, investing, or launching projects they never had time for before. They rediscover curiosity.

The move that started as a financial or lifestyle decision becomes a catalyst for purpose.

You'll find yourself mentoring founders at a co-working space, helping a nonprofit with strategy, or teaching your kids lessons you didn't have bandwidth to teach before. You'll notice how generosity grows when you're not operating on fumes.

That's the real dividend. A surplus of attention you can reinvest in what matters.

Living in Alignment

Freedom isn't a finish line. It's maintenance. It's daily alignment between values and actions.

Some mornings you'll get it wrong. You'll let the calendar fill too fast or fall back into old habits. That's normal. The difference now is aware-ness. You can see misalignment faster and correct it sooner.

The frameworks in this book are meant to be revisited, not remembered.

Pull them out when life feels heavy. Run a new ROI calculation when priorities shift. Rebuild your Network Flywheel when curiosity fades. Realign your Freedom Metrics when pace overtakes purpose.

Each concept is a lever you can pull again whenever you need to recalibrate.

The Responsibility of Freedom

With freedom comes stewardship.

Florida has become a magnet for leaders and capital, which means the culture you create here matters. Every executive who relocates adds a new strand to the state's future.

Model balance. Model generosity. Model integrity. Show that success can look calm and decisive at the same time.

If you treat your freedom as an asset to share, the ecosystem strengthens around you.

That's how better communities, and better companies, are built.

A Final Story

A friend of mine, a retired software founder, once told me, "Florida is the only place I've lived where I measure days by conversations, not meetings."

He spends mornings on calls with founders, afternoons on the water, and evenings cooking with his wife. He said he's never been busier in the right ways.

That sentence captures the essence of the Freedom Dividend: busy in the right ways.

The kind of busy that fills you instead of empties you.

Your Ongoing ROI

Keep a small notebook or digital file called "Freedom Metrics."

Once a quarter, jot down three reflections:

1. What gave me energy this season?
2. What drained it?
3. What changed for the better because I designed it?

Those notes become your new financials. A personal balance sheet of fulfillment.

When the wins pile up quietly, that's growth.

When you catch yourself smiling mid-morning for no reason, that's profit.

Passing It Forward

At some point, another executive will call you with the same question you once had:

"How did you make the move work?"

Hand them this mindset. Tell them the truth; that relocation is part logistics and part self-discovery. That Florida isn't an escape; it's an experiment in alignment. That the real ROI isn't lower taxes but higher clarity.

The more you share what you've learned, the stronger your own system becomes. Teaching is reinforcement.

That's how freedom compounds. Not just personally, but communally.

A Closing Thought

If you've built the systems, aligned the calendars, chosen the market, and found your rhythm, then you've already succeeded.

Now the work is to live it. To let the days flow instead of forcing them, to keep refining the design one decision at a time.

You didn't move to slow down. You moved to live intentionally. To work when you choose, rest when you need, and build things that outlast you.

That's the Freedom Dividend. A life that pays you back in time, health, and purpose.

Welcome home!

ACKNOWLEDGMENTS

Gratitude to every founder, operator, and executive who trusted me with their stories of transition. This book grew out of those conversations; late-night calls, conference hallways, coffee meetups, and candid reflections about what it really takes to rebuild a life while running a business.

To my friends and family, who made Florida home long before I did, and who reminded me that freedom isn't a destination, it's a daily design.

And to every professional who decides to take the leap south - may this book save you a few mistakes and earn you a few more mornings that start with peace.

ABOUT THE AUTHOR

Joseph Schorr is a tech executive, revenue strategist, and multi-time startup advisor who has helped venture-backed founders and Fortune 500 teams design go-to-market systems that scale.

He serves as Chief Revenue Officer of a cybersecurity company and founder of The Wizzo Group, an advisory firm focused on partnerships, GTM architecture, and solution-led growth.

Joe is also a licensed Real Estate Agent in Florida. After spending thirty years building businesses and networks from Florida's Gulf Coast, he now helps other executives design strategic relocations that optimize for both financial return and quality of life.

Born and raised in Philadelphia (Go Birds!), Joe eventually moved south with his Floridian wife—where, yes, it really is as nice as it looks. His greatest joys are his three kids and his new grandbaby.

Follow Joe on LinkedIn → linkedin.com/in/josephschorr

From the Author

If you found this book helpful, PLEASE consider leaving a short review on Amazon. It helps other executives discover the playbook and gives me insight into what really clicks.

Work With Me on Your Florida Relocation

If this book resonates with you, and you're serious about making your Florida relocation strategic rather than emotional, let's talk!

I work with a small number of executives each year who want:

- **Strategic coordination** across their full relocation (not just real estate)
- **Access to 30 years** of Tampa Bay network and market knowledge
- **An advisor who speaks their language** (equity, domicile, portfolio strategy)
- **Integration support** that goes beyond closing day

I'm selective because this work requires real attention. But for executives who are ready to treat their relocation like the life-changing project it is, I can help you avoid the mistakes, accelerate the timeline, and design for freedom from day one.

The conversation starts simply:

- One strategic call to understand your situation
- Clear assessment of which Florida market fits
- Honest evaluation of timing and readiness
- Decision about whether working together makes sense

No pressure. Just clarity.

To start that conversation:

- Email: Joe@Wizzo.Group
- LinkedIn: LinkedIn.com/in/JosephSchorr

OTHER RESOURCES

WIZZO PRESS PUBLISHES field guides for the current and next chapters of your career… books for operators building smarter lives, not just bigger ones.

Visit **wizzopress.com** for titles in the Wizzo Growth and Wizzo Transitions series:

- "Florida Relocation Workbook" (Companion to this book with expanded exercises)
- "3's Company: Ignite Your Startup's Revenue Engine Through Strategic Partnerships"
- "Rookie Agent's Flywheel- Playbook for Professionals Starting a Second Act in Real Estate" (Coming Soon)
- "Solution Led Growth" (Coming Soon)
- "Watering Hole Sales" (Coming Soon)
- Upcoming titles on partnerships, revenue strategy, and executive transitions
- Free resources and tools for relocating executives

Author's Note

Every company in this book is real or inspired by actual people I've worked with. Some names, details, and scenarios have been adjusted for confidentiality, but the lessons have been lived.

www.ingramcontent.com/pod-product-compliance
Lightning Source LLC
Chambersburg PA
CBHW071553200326
41519CB00021BB/6731